LOVE GOD
AND
DO WHAT YOU PLEASE!

Translated by C. D. McEnniry, C.SS.R.
from the original Italian of
THE PRACTICE OF THE LOVE OF JESUS CHRIST
by St. Alphonsus Liguori

Adapted and edited by
M. J. Huber, C.SS.R.

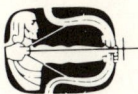

LIGUORIAN BOOKS
Redemptorist Fathers
Liguori, Missouri 63057

Imprimi Potest:
Daniel L. Lowery, C.SS.R.
Provincial, St. Louis Province
Redemptorist Fathers
March 1, 1970

Imprimatur:
St. Louis, March 3, 1970
+ John J. Cardinal Carberry
Archbishop of St. Louis

TABLE OF CONTENTS

TABLE OF CONTENTS

FOREWORD

Everybody is talking love, love, love!

"Love God and Do What You Please!" takes up the challenge to love, to love without limit, but to love in a way that brings happiness never-ending.

This book was written about 200 years ago by St. Alphonsus Liguori, the founder of the Redemptorist missionary congregation.

In the writings of St. Alphonsus there is a distinct flavor of what is known in our day as personalist religion: "God and me!" But his personal love of God led St. Alphonsus to a boundless love of his fellow men. He was a pioneer in his time in what we speak of as getting involved with the minorities and the disadvantaged. He founded his missionary congregation to work for the neglected people living in the hills outside the cities, people who were without priests, people who were practically starved for religious guidance.

St. Alphonsus wanted all God's children to burn with the spirit of Christ. In bringing the good news of Christ to his fellow men he made a vow never to waste a moment of time. Truly the motto of his life might well have been not just "God and me!" but "For God and for the world!"

No matter whether we talk about commitment, dedication, involvement, apostolate or simply working for God and for our neighbor, the fulfillment we find in living as total Christians depends upon our personal union with Christ and our love for God.

"For the Lord has said, 'He who abides in me, and I in him, he bears much fruit: for without me you can do nothing'" (John 15:5) — Decree on the Apostolate of the Laity, No. 4.

"Indeed the law of love, which is the Lord's greatest commandment, impels all the faithful to promote God's glory through the spread of His kingdom and to obtain for all men that eternal life which consists in knowing the only true God and Him whom He sent, Jesus Christ" — Decree on the Apostolate of the Laity, No. 3.

—M. J. Huber, C.SS.R.

CHAPTER I

I HAVE LOVED YOU AS LONG
AS I HAVE BEEN GOD

"Love God," said St. Augustine, "and do what you please."

If you love God sincerely, the only thing that will please you is doing God's will.

All holiness and perfection consists in loving Jesus Christ, our God, our highest good and our Savior. "Whoever loves me," says Jesus himself, "will be loved by my eternal Father."

"Some," says St. Francis de Sales, "place perfection in austerity of life, others in prayer, others in receiving the sacraments frequently, others in almsgiving; but they deceive themselves. Perfection consists in loving God with all your heart."

The apostle writes: "Above all . . . have love which is the bond of perfection" (Col. 3:14). It is love that unites and preserves all the virtues and makes man perfect. That is why St. Augustine said: "Love, and do what you please: love God, and then do whatever you like; because, when a soul loves God, that very love teaches it to avoid everything that displeases God and to do everything that pleases Him."

And does God not deserve all our love? He has loved us from all eternity: "I have loved you with an everlasting love" (Jer. 31:3). "See, O man," says the Lord, "how I have been the first to love you. You were not yet in the world, the world itself did not exist, but even then I loved you. As long as I have been God I have loved you."

EVERYTHING SPEAKS OF LOVE

Seeing that men are drawn by gifts, God used gifts to draw them to His love. That is why He said: "I will draw them . . . by the bonds of love" (Osee 11:4).

It is for this purpose that God has given all His gifts to man. God has given man a soul; an imagination, a memory, an intellect and a will; He has given him a body with its senses. God has created heaven and earth and so many other things — all for the love of man. The heavens, the stars, the planets, the seas, the rivers, the springs, the mountains, the plains, metals, fruits, animals — all these He has created for the benefit of man, that man might be moved by gratitude to love the Giver of so many gifts.

"Heaven and earth and all things," says St. Augustine, "bid me love You. My Lord, everything I see in the world, everything speaks to me and exhorts me to love You, because everything tells me You have made it for love of me."

Abbot Rance, founder of the Trappist monks, whenever he paused in his solitude to gaze upon the hills and the springs and the birds and the flowers and the planets and the heavens, felt himself inspired to love the God who had created them for love of Him.

So too, St. Mary Magdalen of Pazzi, whenever she held in her hand a beautiful flower, would feel excited to love God and would say: "From all eternity my Lord has thought of creating this flower for love of me."

St. Teresa when looking at trees or springs or brooks or lakes or meadows, would say that all these beautiful things gently scolded her for her ingratitude in loving so little the Creator who had made them in order to win her love.

When a certain hermit went walking through the fields, it seemed to him that the blades of grass and the flowers he saw on the way would scold him for his ingratitude toward God, and so he would strike them with a stick he carried saying: "Be quiet, be quiet! You call me ungrateful. You tell me that God has created you for love of me and still I do not love Him. I hear you. Be quiet, stop scolding."

HE GAVE HIMSELF

But God was not content with giving us all these beautiful creatures. In order to win our love He gave us himself. The eternal Father has gone so far as to give us His own and only Son. "God so loved the world as to give his only-begotten Son" (John 3:16). For the immense love He bore us, He sent His beloved Son to make satisfaction for us and thus restore to us the life which sin had taken away. "For the too great love wherewith he loved us and when we were dead in sin, he made us live in Christ" (Eph. 2:4-5). And giving us His Son, He has given us every good, His grace, His love, His heaven; for all these gifts are certainly less than the gift of His Son. "He who has not spared even his own Son but has delivered him for us all, how can he fail to grant us also all things with him?" (Rom. 8:33)

In the same manner the Son, for the love He bears us, gave himself entirely to us. "He loved us and gave himself up for us" (Eph. 5:2). In order to save us from eternal death and to allow us to regain the divine grace and the heaven which we had lost, He became Man and clothed himself in flesh like us: "And the Word was made flesh" (John 1:14).

So we see a God dispossessing himself: "He dispossessed himself taking the form of a servant . . . and in appearance he was found as a man." The Lord of the world humbled himself to such a degree as to take the form of a servant and to submit to all the miseries which men endure.

What astounds us more is the fact that He could have saved us without dying and without suffering; but no, He chose an afflicted and lowly life and a painful and shameful death, even death on a cross — the infamous death reserved for criminals: "He humbled himself, being made obedient unto death, even unto the death of the cross" (Phil. 2:8). He loved us, and because He loved us He gave himself up to suffering and shame and to a death more painful than any man has ever suffered on this earth.

Such was the love of Jesus for men that it made Him long for the hour of His death that He might give them a proof of the love He bore them. "I have a baptism wherewith I am to be baptized, and how distressed I am until it be accomplished!" (Luke 12:50) "I am to be baptized with my own blood, and how I long for the hour of my passion to come quickly that man may see the love I bear him!"

HIS HOUR

St. John, writing of that night in which Jesus began His suffering, says: "Jesus, knowing that his hour was come that he should pass out of this world to the Father, having loved his own . . . he loved them unto the end" (John 13:1). The Redeemer called that hour His hour; because the hour of His death was the hour of His desires; it was then He wished to give to men the final proof of His love, dying for them upon a cross, consumed with anguish.

When love wants to make itself known, it goes looking not for what befits its dignity, but for what will best manifest it to the beloved.

If faith had not taught it, who could have ever believed that a God, almighty, supremely happy, and Lord of all things, should have willed to love man so much?

Venerable John d'Avila was so deeply enamored of Jesus Christ that he never preached a sermon without dwelling upon the love Jesus Christ bears us. In one of his treatises on the love of this most loving Redeemer for men he writes these burning words:

"So have You loved man, O my Redeemer, that whoever thinks of this love cannot help loving You. Your love overwhelms our hearts, as the apostle says: 'The love . . . of Christ impels us!' The source of Jesus Christ's love for men is His love for God. Therefore He says at the Last Supper on Holy Thursday night: 'That the world may know that I love the Father, arise, let us go.' But go where? To die on the cross for men!

"The intellect cannot succeed in comprehending how this fire burns in the heart of Jesus Christ. If, instead of one death, He had been commanded to suffer a thousand deaths, His love was great enough to accept them all. And if He had been told to suffer for one man alone what He suffered for all, He would have done for each singly what He has done for all together. He hung for three hours on the cross, but had it been necessary to hang there till the day of judgment, He had love enough to do it. Thus we see that Jesus Christ loved much more than He suffered. O love divine, how much greater you were than you appeared! You appeared great externally because so many wounds and bruises tell of a great love, but they do not tell all its greatness. There was much more hidden than appeared, for this was but a spark escaping from that great fire of immense love.

"This is the greatest sign of love, to give one's life for one's friends; but this sign did not suffice for Jesus Christ to express His love.

"O Thief of hearts, Your love has crushed even our hard hearts! You have set the whole world on fire with Your love! O Lord, when I look at the cross, everything pleads for my love. Your love begs me to love You and never to forget You."

THINK OF CHRIST'S SUFFERINGS

Devotion to the passion of Jesus Christ is a most useful and consoling way of learning to love God. From the passion of Jesus Christ we receive so many treasures: hope of pardon, strength in temptation, assurance of paradise. Where do we find so much light of truth, so many loving appeals, so many inspirations to change our life, so many desires to give ourselves to God, if not in the sufferings of Jesus Christ?

St. Bonaventure says there is no devotion more adapted to sanctify a soul than meditation on the passion of Jesus Christ; therefore he counsels us to meditate daily on the passion if we wish to advance in divine love. "If you wish to make progress meditate daily on the Lord's passion, for nothing produces complete sanctity in the soul as does meditation on the passion of Christ." And before him St. Augustine had said that one tear shed in memory of the passion is more meritorious than a weekly fast on bread and water.

The saints are always occupied in reflecting on the sufferings of Jesus Christ. It was by this means that St. Francis of Assisi became a seraph. One day he was discovered shedding tears and sobbing loudly. When asked the reason he replied: "I am weeping over the sufferings and the ignominies of Our Lord. And what pains me most is that men for whom He suffered so much live forgetful of His passion." Whenever the saint heard the bleating of a lamb or saw anything else that recalled the memory of the suffering of Jesus he immediately began to weep. One day when he was ill somebody suggested reading to him from a pious book. "My book," he replied, "is Jesus crucified."

PRAYER

O Lord Jesus, You spent 33 years in sweat and labor, You gave Your blood and Your life to save men. In a word, You spared nothing to make Yourself loved; and how is it possible that there are men who know all this and still do not love You? O God, I am one of these ungrateful persons. I see the wrong I have done. Jesus, have mercy on me! I offer You my ungrateful heart – ungrateful, but repentant. Yes, I do repent, my dear Redeemer, for having despised You. I repent, and I love You with my whole heart.

My soul, love a God bound like a criminal for your sake, a God scourged for you, a God made a mock king for you, a God dead on a tree of shame for you.

Yes, my Savior, my God, I love You, I love You! Make me remember always how much You have suffered for me, that I may never again forget to love You.

O Mary, refuge of sinners and Mother of my Savior, help a sinner who wishes to love God and who recommends himself to you; help me for the love you bear to Jesus Christ!

CHAPTER II

I HAVE NEVER STOPPED LOVING YOU

"Jesus, knowing that his hour was come that he should pass out of this world to his Father, having loved his own . . . he loved them unto the end" (John 13:1).

Our loving Savior, knowing that the moment had come to leave this world, wished, before going to die for us, to leave us the greatest proof that He could give us of the love He bore us — and that was the gift of the Blessed Sacrament.

St. Bernardine of Siena says that the proofs of love given at death are remembered more vividly and held more dear. Therefore friends, when dying, are wont to leave to those they loved in life some gift, a garment, a ring, in memory of their affection. But You, O my Jesus, on leaving this world, what have You left us in memory of Your love? Not a garment, or a ring: no, You have left us Your entire self. "He gave you all," says St. John Chrysostom, "He left nothing for himself."

In this gift of the Eucharist Jesus Christ wished to pour out all the riches of the love He had kept in reserve for men. St. Paul says that Jesus willed to give this great gift to men precisely on that night in which men were planning His death. "The Lord Jesus, the same night in which he was betrayed, took bread, and giving thanks, broke and said: 'This is my body' " (1 Cor. 11:23-24). St. Bernardine of Siena says that Jesus Christ, burning with love for us and not even content to go out and die for us, was impelled, before dying, by the excess of His love, to do something surpassing anything that had ever been done before — to give His own body for us to eat.

St. Thomas calls this sacrament "sacrament of love, pledge of love." *Sacrament of love* because it was love alone that induced Jesus Christ to give us in the Eucharist His entire self. *Pledge of love* because, if we had ever doubted His love, we have in this sacrament a pledge of it. As if our Redeemer, in leaving us this gift, had said: "Dear children, if ever you have doubted My love, behold, I leave you Myself in this sacrament. With such a pledge as a reminder, you can never again doubt that I love you, and that I love you dearly."

PLEDGE OF GLORY

The Eucharist is not only a pledge of the love of Jesus Christ, it is also a pledge of the heaven He wills to give us. St. Philip Neri knew no other name for Jesus Christ in this sacrament except *love*. Thus when they brought him the holy Viaticum he was heard exclaiming: "Oh, there is my love! Give me my love!"

Who could have ever imagined, if He had not actually done it, that the incarnate Word would have hidden himself under the appearance of bread in order to become our food?

When Jesus Christ revealed to His disciples this sacrament which He promised to leave them, many could not believe it, and they abandoned Him saying: "How can this man give us his flesh to eat?" (John 6:53) "This is a hard saying: who can accept it?" (John 6:61). But what men could not believe, the great love of Jesus Christ has done. "Take ye, and eat," He said to His disciples; and through them to all of us, before He went out to die.

With what longing Jesus Christ yearns to come to our souls in Holy Communion! "With desire have I desired to eat this Pasch with you" (Luke 22:15). Thus He spoke on that night in which He instituted this sacrament of love. "With desire have I desired."

It was, says St. Lawrence Justinian, His immense love which forced Him to say this. And in order that everybody might be able to receive Him with ease, He wished to leave himself under the appearance of bread. If He had left himself under the appearance of some rare or costly food, the poor would have been excluded. But no! Jesus has willed to place himself under the appearance of bread, a food that costs little and is found everywhere so that everybody, in every country, might be able to find Him and receive Him.

And then, to make sure that we really do receive Him, not only does He invite us to receive Him in Holy Communion; He also imposes it upon us as a command: "Take ye, and eat; this is my body." To induce us to receive Him He draws us with the promise of heaven: "He that eats my flesh has life everlasting" (John 6:55). "He who eats this bread will live forever" (John 6:59). He even threatens us by declaring excluded from paradise all who refuse to communicate: "Except you eat the flesh of the Son of man, you shall not have life in you" (John 6:54). These invitations, these promises, all arise from the great desire He has to come to us in this sacrament.

But why does Jesus Christ so ardently desire that we should receive Him in Holy Communion? Here is the reason. "Love," says St. Denis, "aspires to, and tends toward union." And St. Thomas says: "Two who love each other desire to become one." Two friends who love each other from the bottom of their heart, would wish to be so closely united as to form but one person. Now this is why the immense love which God bears to men has caused Him, not only to give himself entirely to them in the eternal kingdom, but to allow men, even here on this earth, to possess Him in the closest possible union, by giving them His entire self in this sacrament. We do not see Him, but He sees us, and He is there really present. He is present, to let us possess Him; but He is hidden, to make us yearn for Him; and so long as we are exiled from our fatherland, Jesus wills to give himself entirely to us and to be intimately united with us.

TO EACH ONE OF US

He could not satisfy His love by giving himself entirely to the whole human race in His incarnation and in His dying for all men. No, He wished to find a way of giving himself to each one of us. Therefore did He institute the Sacrament of the Altar, where He can in fact unite himself with each one of us. "He who eats my flesh abides in me and I in him" (John 6:57). In Holy Communion Jesus unites himself with the soul and the soul unites itself with Jesus; and this union is not merely affective; it is real. St. Francis de Sales said: "Nowhere do we find our Savior more tender or more loving than here where He, so to speak, annihilates himself and reduces himself to food in order to penetrate our souls and to unite himself to the hearts of His friends." And St. John Chrysostom says that Jesus Christ, for the burning love He bore us, wished to unite himself so closely to us that we should become one and the same with Him — "for such is the dream of true lovers."

"You have willed," adds St. Lawrence Justinian, "O God enamored of our souls, that by means of this sacrament, Your heart and our heart should become but one heart inseparably united."

St. Bernardine of Siena says that Jesus Christ's giving himself to us as food was the highest degree of love, because He gave himself to us to unite himself completely with us, just as food is united with him who eats it. How Jesus is pleased to be united to our souls!

We should be convinced that a soul can neither do nor imagine anything more pleasing to Jesus Christ than to communicate with the dispositions proper for one who is receiving such a Guest into his heart; for thus he unites himself to Jesus Christ. I said "with the *proper* dispositions," not with the dispositions *worthy* of such a Guest, for if such dispositions were demanded, who could ever communicate? Only a God would be *worthy* to receive a God. By "proper" dispositions I mean those proper to a human being.

The dispositions required for frequent reception of Holy Communion are:

1. To be in the state of grace, to the best of our knowledge.

2. To have a good intention in communicating.

These two dispositions are necessary, but these two are also sufficient, though there is no limit put to the nobility of disposition we may and should strive to have. But as long as we have these two dispositions, the reception of Holy Communion will be more profitable than the abstaining from it.

STATE OF GRACE

Consider these two dispositions more particularly. The first requisite is the *state of grace.* What do we mean by this? It does not mean that we must have been constantly in the state of grace — so that we must be for a long time free from grievous sin. But, at the time we receive, we must be free from grievous sin. A good confession and the determination never to commit grievous sin in the future, is the best guarantee for that.

It does not mean exactly either that your conscience must be calm and peaceful — so that, if you have a vague and indefinite fear of being unworthy or of being in the state of sin, you must abstain from Communion. No! So long as you are not certain of having committed a grievous sin since your last good confession, you are worthy to go to Holy Communion.

Nor does it mean that you must go to confession before every Communion. You are obliged to go to confession before Holy Communion, if you have committed a grievous sin since your last good confession, and only then. True, it is good to make it a practice to go to confession every few weeks or once a month; but in case you are unable to get to confession and are not certain of being in the state of sin, take the opportunity that presents itself of going to Holy Communion.

Our Lord teaches us that this disposition is required for Holy Communion by the very fact that He instituted it in the form of a food for our soul. Food is of no use to a dead man; it is only the living who can profit by it. Now, the life of the soul is sanctifying grace — the freedom from mortal sin.

RIGHT INTENTION

The second disposition required is: *to have a right intention in receiving.* What do we mean by a right intention? A right intention — as the Decree of Pope Pius X on Holy Communion says — consists in this: that he who approaches the holy table should do so not out of routine or vainglory or human respect, but for the purpose of pleasing God, of being more closely united with Him by charity, and of seeking this divine remedy for his weaknesses and defects.

It does not mean that if another motive, human and imperfect, creeps in as a secondary motive for going to Holy Communion, that one's intention is no longer right. For instance, a person may really be prompted by a desire of being better when going to Holy Communion and then a little vainglory slips in, or a little desire to please, or compliance with custom; this does not make the main purpose cease to be right.

It does not mean that I must explicitly formulate these motives before Holy Communion. The mere fact of approaching the holy table freely is a proof that you are moved thereto by faith and confidence, by a desire to become better, or by love for Our Lord.

Nor does it mean that I must have all the right intentions mentioned in the Pope's decree. If I have one of them, if I simply communicate in order to become better, it is sufficient.

That this disposition is necessary, is clear once more from the purpose for which Our Lord instituted the Blessed Sacrament. It is to be for us a means of preserving the life of our soul — to give us the strength of soul necessary to avoid sin. We must use all things for the purpose for which Our Lord gives them to us.

These two conditions — to be in the state of grace, to the best of our knowledge, and to have a right intention — are necessary and sufficient for receiving Holy Communion, whether once a year or every week or every day. More is not demanded. Naturally, the better our dispositions, the more we will profit by the graces of this sacrament. But so long as we have these two dispositions, Communion in itself will be more profitable than the omission of it. So long as we receive worthily, better an imperfect Communion than no Communion; and every Communion will help us to be better for the next one.

There is nothing from which we can draw such profit as from Holy Communion. The eternal Father has made Jesus Christ Master of all His divine riches: ". . . the Father had given him all things into his hands" (John 13:3). Therefore when Jesus comes into a soul in Holy Communion, He brings with Him immense treasures of graces.

Communion is a powerful antidote which frees us from venial sins and preserves us from serious sins. We say "frees us from venial sins" because, according to St. Thomas, by means of this sacrament a man is moved to make acts of love whereby his venial sins are forgiven. We say "preserves us from serious sins" because Communion confers an increase of grace that prevents us from falling into grave faults. Innocent III wrote that Jesus Christ, by His passion, freed us from the power of sin, but by the Eucharist He freed us from the power of sinning.

The principal effect of this sacrament is to inflame us with divine love. God is love. Now it is precisely this fire of love which the Son of God came to kindle on earth. "I am come to cast fire upon the earth." And He adds that He longs for nothing more than to see that blessed fire kindled in our souls. "And what do I desire except that it be kindled?" (Luke 12:49)

Someone will say: "I do not communicate often because I find myself so cold in divine love." The answer: "And so, because you feel cold, you stay away from the fire! On the contrary, precisely because you feel cold should you approach this sacrament more often, if only you desire to love Jesus Christ." "Even though you be lukewarm," says St. Bonaventure, "nevertheless approach this sacrament; the sicker a man feels, the more he needs the doctor." In the same strain writes St. Francis de Sales: "Two kinds of persons should communicate frequently: the perfect to stay perfect, the imperfect to become perfect."

Our Lord said one day to St. Matilda: "When you go to Communion, desire all the love for Me of which a human heart is capable, and I will accept your love as though it were really such."

PRAYER

O God of love, O infinite Lover, worthy of infinite love, tell me, is there anything else You could possibly do to make Yourself loved by us? You were not satisfied to become Man and submit to all our miseries. You were not satisfied to shed all Your blood for us in the midst of torments and then to die consumed by sufferings on a cross reserved for criminals. You have abased Yourself so far as to hide under the appearance of bread in order to become our food and to unite Yourself entirely to each one of us. Tell me, is there anything else You could possibly invent to make Yourself loved? What open doors to happiness we pass by, if in this life we do not learn to love You!

My Jesus, I do not want to die without having loved You very much.

I regret to think that I have caused You so much displeasure; I repent of all my sins, and I will never again offend You.

Now I love You more than all things. I consecrate to You all my affections. Give me always a greater desire to love You and give me also the strength to fulfill my desire.

O Mother of God, Mary, pray to Jesus for me.

CHAPTER III

PUT YOUR HAND IN MINE AND TRUST ME

David placed all his hope of salvation in his future Redeemer and said: "Into Your hands I commend my spirit; You will redeem me, O Lord, O faithful God." How much more should we put all our hope in Jesus Christ, now that He has come into the world and completed the work of redemption! With greater confidence than David each one of us should say and keep on saying: "Into Your hands I commend my spirit; You will redeem me, O Lord, O faithful God."

If we have great reason to fear eternal death on account of the offenses we have committed against God, we have still stronger reasons to hope for eternal life through the merits of Jesus Christ; for these merits have infinitely more power to save us than our sins have to condemn us. We indeed have sinned and by our sins deserved punishment, but the Redeemer has come to take upon himself our sins and to satisfy for them by His sufferings. "Surely He has borne our infirmities and carried our sorrows" (Is. 53:4).

"Blotting out the handwriting of the decree that was against us . . . He has taken the same out of the way, fastening it to the cross" (Col. 2:14). He canceled with His blood the decree of our condemnation, and then He fastened it to the cross, so that every time we see our sentence of condemnation for the sins committed, we may at the same time see the cross whereon Jesus Christ, dying, canceled it with His blood, and so reawaken our hope of pardon and eternal salvation.

How much better the blood of Jesus Christ pleads for us and obtains for us the divine pardon, than the blood of Abel cried out against Cain! "You have come . . . to Jesus, the mediator of the New Testament, and to the sprinkling of blood which speaks better than that of Abel" (Heb. 12:24). As though the apostle had said: "O sinners, happy you, who after your sin have had recourse to Jesus crucified, who has shed all His blood in order to become mediator of peace between sinners and God and to obtain pardon for them! Your sins indeed cry out against you, but the blood of the Redeemer pleads in your favor, and at the voice of this blood, divine justice cannot but be placated."

HE DIED FOR US

It is true that we must render a rigorous account of all our sins to the divine Judge. But who is it that will be our judge? "The Father . . . hath given all judgment to the Son" (John 5:22). Let us take heart; the eternal Father has committed the office of judging us to no other than our Redeemer. Therefore St. Paul encourages us saying: "Who is it that shall condemn us when Christ Jesus who died . . . is pleading for us?" (Rom. 8:34) Who is the judge? It is that same Savior who, in order not to condemn us to eternal death, has condemned himself and has died; and, not content with that, He continues, even today in heaven, to plead with His Father for our salvation.

St. Thomas of Villanova writes: "Sinner, if you repent of your sins, what do you fear? How will He condemn you who died so that He would not have to condemn you? How will He drive you away when you return to His feet, He who came down from heaven to go in search of you even while you were running from Him!"

And if, on account of our weakness, we fear to fall in the attacks of that enemy whom we must continually fight, here, as the apostle warns us, is what we must do. " . . . put aside every encumbrance and the sin entangling us, and run with patience to the fight set before us, looking toward the author and finisher of faith, Jesus, who, for the joy set before him, endured a cross, despising shame . . . " (Heb. 12:1-2). Then let us go forward with courage to the battle, with our eyes fixed on Jesus crucified, who from the cross offers His aid, the victory and the crown.

In the past we have fallen because we stopped looking on the wounds and the ignominies suffered by our Savior, and so we failed to call on Him for help. But for the future, if we remember how much He has suffered for our love, and how He is always prompt to help us if we have recourse to Him, surely we shall not be defeated by our enemies.

HOPE AND LOVE

What two great mysteries of hope and of love we find in the passion of Jesus Christ and in the Sacrament of the Altar! Mysteries so great that, if faith had not revealed them, who could ever have believed them? An omnipotent God, willing to make himself Man, to shed all His blood, and to die in agony on a cross! And why? To pay the price of our sins and to save us! And then He was willing to give His body, once sacrificed for us on the cross, to be our food, and thus to unite himself entirely to us! How these two mysteries should consume the hearts of all men with love!

"Let us go with confidence to the throne of grace, that we may obtain mercy and find grace in seasonable aid" (Heb. 4:16). This throne of grace is the cross where Jesus hangs to dispense grace and mercy to everyone that has recourse to Him. But it is urgent that we have recourse to Him at once, while we can get the help we need to save our souls; otherwise the day may come when we shall no longer be able to find Him. Let us go with great confidence. No discouragement on account of our sins! In Jesus Christ crucified we shall find every grace. "In all things you are made rich in him . . . so that nothing is wanting to you in any grace" (1 Cor. 1:5-7). The merits of Jesus Christ have made us rich in all divine treasures and have made us capable of receiving every grace we desire.

HE GAVE US ALL THINGS

See how Our Lord teaches us the way to obtain whatever we wish from the eternal Father. "Amen, amen, I say unto you, if you ask the Father anything in my name, he will give it to you" (John 16:23). Ask My Father in My name whatever you desire, and I promise that He will hear you. For how could the Father ever refuse us any other gift, since He has given us His well-beloved and only-begotten Son? "He that spared not even his own son, but delivered him up for us all, how has he not also with him given us all things?" (Rom. 8:32) The apostle said "all things"; therefore nothing is excluded – not pardon, not perseverance, not holy love, not perfection, not paradise. He gave us *all* things. But we must ask. God is lavish in giving to everyone that asks.

Here I wish to add some beautiful citations from the writings of Father d'Avila regarding the great confidence we should have in the merits of Jesus Christ. He says:

"Let us never forget that between the eternal Father and us stands the Mediator, Jesus Christ, through whom we are bound to the Father by such strong bonds of love that they can never be broken except by serious sin. Sinners who are lost, are lost not because there was no atonement for their sins, but because they refused to make use of the sacraments and thus share in the atonement offered by Jesus Christ.

"Jesus said to his Father: 'Father, I will that wherever I am, those also, whom thou hast given to me, should be with with me' (John 17:24). And so, forgiven and loved, we are certain of never being abandoned. The Lord said through Isaiah: 'Can a woman forget her infant? And if she should forget, yet will I never forget you. Behold I have graven you in my hands' (Is. 49:15-16). He has written us on His hands with His own blood. Therefore we should let nothing disturb us, since everything is managed by those hands which were nailed to the cross in testimony of the love He bears us.

"Let my sins surround me, let fears for the future assail me. It will not matter. I will invoke Jesus Christ, who is all merciful, who loved me even unto death, and I will take heart. My soul is so precious that a God has delivered himself up for me.

"If you believe that the eternal Father has given you His Son, then believe that He will give you everything else. Never imagine that Jesus Christ has forgotten you — He who has left, as a remembrance of His love, the richest of all pledges, His own very self in the Sacrament of the Altar."

PRAYER

My Jesus, how Your suffering fills me with holy hope! How could I ever fear that I should not receive the pardon of my sins and every necessary grace from an almighty God who has given me His life?

My Jesus, my hope and my love! You have preferred to lose Your life rather than lose me.

I love You above all things, my Redeemer and my God. You have given yourself entirely to me; I give You my will. I love You, I love You; and I wish always to repeat: I love You, I love You. So I wish to speak during life, so I wish to speak at the hour of my death, that the last sound from my dying lips may be these words: My God, I love You. From that moment I shall begin to love You with an unending love and go on forever without the danger of ever ceasing to love You.

I love You, and because I love You, I repent of having offended You.

My dear Redeemer, I firmly hope to receive from You eternal salvation in the life to come, and in this life, perseverance in Your love. Give me perseverance in praying to You.

This same favor of persevering in prayer I ask and hope from you, Mary, my Queen.

CHAPTER IV

LOVE ME AND DO WHAT YOU PLEASE

Jesus Christ, being God, has a right to all our love; but by the love He has shown us, He has willed, as it were, to compel us to love Him, at least out of gratitude for all He has done and suffered for us. He has loved us dearly that we might love Him dearly. "Why does God love if not to be loved?" asks St. Bernard. The first commandment He gave us was this: "You shall love the Lord your God with your whole heart" (Deut. 6:5).

And St. Paul says: "Love is the fulfilling of the law" (Rom. 13:10). The Greek text has, instead of "the fulfilling of the law," "the embracing of the law." Love embraces the entire law.

But why do we need a law commanding us to love God? How can we ever refrain from loving a God whom we see fastened to a cross and dying for love of us?

How well pleased is Jesus Christ when we frequently recall His passion!

St. Thomas of Villanova said, "Look at that cross, look at those sufferings and that bitter death which Jesus Christ suffered for you; after so many and such great proofs of His love, you can no longer doubt that He loves you and loves you much."

In the great mystery of human redemption we find a striking proof of the determination and the concern of Jesus Christ to find many ways to make himself loved. To die for our salvation, it would have sufficed to die with the Holy Innocents massacred by Herod. But, no! He willed first to live a life of 33 years full of hardships and trials. During this life, in order to draw us to His love, He willed to show himself to us under various forms. First, He showed himself as a poor infant in a manger, then as a boy in a workshop, and finally as a condemned criminal on a cross. Before dying on that cross, He willed to be seen under various pitiable appearances: sweating blood in an agony in the garden, torn by whips in the praetorium of Pilate, scoffed at as a mock king, with a stick in His hand, a purple rag over His shoulders, and a crown of thorns on His head, dragged through the public streets carrying His cross, and finally suspended by nails from the cross on Calvary. Tell me, does He, or does He not, deserve to be loved, a God who has suffered so many torments and tried in so many ways to win our love?

St. John Chrysostom tells what divine love does for the soul: "Once the love of God has taken possession of a soul, it produces in that soul an insatiable desire to work for the Beloved, so that, no matter how many or what great things it accomplishes, or how much time it spends in their accomplishment, all seems nothing, and it is always lamenting that it does so little for God. Taught by love how much God deserves, it sees clearly the defects in its actions; it feels only confusion and regret, realizing that they are all too insignificant for so great a God."

How sadly he deceives himself, says St. Francis de Sales, who thinks to find holiness in anything else but in loving God! Some, he writes, place perfection in austerity of life, others in almsgiving, others in prayer, others in receiving the sacraments. I, for my part, know of no other perfection than that of loving God with my whole heart. Because all the other virtues, without love, are nothing. And if we do not possess the fullness of this divine love, the fault is our own; we have never resolved once and for all to give ourselves entirely to God.

ONE THING NECESSARY

One day the Lord said to St. Teresa: "Whatever is not done for Me is worthless." If we could only grasp this great truth: "But one thing is necessary." It is not necessary to be rich in this world's goods; it is not necessary to stand high in the esteem of our fellow men; not necessary to enjoy an easy life, to attain to high office, to be famous as a scholar. One thing only is necessary — to love God and do His will.

We have then one thing, and one thing only, to do — to acquire a true love for Jesus Christ. The masters of the spiritual life tell us the signs by which we can know whether our love is a true love.

Love is generous, because trusting solely in God, it does not hesitate to undertake great things for Him.

Love is strong — strong to crush all evil inclinations, even in the face of the most violent temptations and in the darkest desolation.

Love is obedient. It promptly follows the divine requests.

Love is pure, because it loves only God, and only because He deserves love.

Love is ardent, because it wishes to inflame all men and see them consumed by divine love.

Love is a bond uniting the will of the creature with that of its Creator.

' Love is a longing of the soul to leave this world and unite itself perfectly to God in heaven, there to love Him forever.

But nobody shows us more clearly the qualities of true love and how it should be practiced than that great preacher of love, St. Paul. "If I should have all faith, so that I could remove mountains, and have not love, I am nothing. And if I should distribute all my goods to feed the poor, and if I should deliver my body to be burned, and I have not love, it profits me nothing." The apostle then enumerates the signs of true love and tells us how to practice those virtues that are the daughters of love.

"Charity is patient, is kind; charity does not envy, is not pretentious, is not puffed up, is not ambitious, is not self-seeking, is not provoked; thinks no evil, does not rejoice over wickedness, but rejoices with the truth; bears with all things, believes all things, hopes all things, endures all things" (1 Cor. 13:4-7).

We shall now proceed to consider whether we have the love we should have for Jesus Christ, and to learn what virtues we should especially practice in order to preserve and increase that holy love.

PRAYER

O most lovable and most loving heart of Jesus, unhappy the heart that does not love You! O God, for love of men You died on a cross, deprived of all solace. How can men live so forgetful of You?

O my Jesus, how few are they who love You! I too have gone on for so many years forgetful of You, and therefore I have offended You! My dear Redeemer, I am sorry, not so much on account of the punishment I have deserved as on account of the love You have borne me.

I love You, my Jesus, I love You, and I will love You always.

Never permit me to leave You or to lose You again!

Make me all your own; do it by the merits of Your passion, I beg You. For this I firmly hope.

I have great confidence in your intercession also, Mary, my Queen. Make me love Jesus Christ; and make me love you, my Mother and my hope.

CHAPTER V

LOVE IS ALWAYS PATIENT

Our true and lasting home is heaven, where God has prepared for us eternal rest and joy. In comparison with eternity, our life on earth is very brief, but during that short time of trial we have many things to suffer.

On the day of judgment, in order to receive the reward of eternal happiness, our life must be found conformable to the life of Jesus Christ. For this purpose the eternal Word came into this world, to teach us by His example how to carry the crosses God sends us. "Christ suffered for us, leaving you an example, that you should follow his steps" (1 Peter 2:21). Jesus Christ wished to suffer in order to give us courage in our sufferings.

The life of Jesus Christ was a life of ignominy and pain. The prophet called our Redeemer "despised and the most abject of men, a man of sorrows" (Isaiah 53:3). Despised and treated as the least of men, a man of sorrows! Yes, because the life of Jesus Christ was filled with sufferings and sorrows.

WHOM THE LORD LOVES

As God has treated His beloved Son, so also does He treat everyone that He loves and receives as a son. "For whom the Lord loves he chastises, and he scourges every son whom he receives" (Heb. 12:6). One day the Lord said to St. Teresa: "I want you to know that the souls that are dearest to My Father are the souls afflicted by the greatest sufferings." Therefore, whenever she was in pain, she was wont to declare that she would not exchange her cross for all the treasures of the world. After her death she appeared to someone and revealed that she enjoyed a great reward in heaven, not so much for the good works she had performed, as for the sufferings she had willingly borne for the love of God, and that, if anything could make her wish to return to this world, it would be the desire to suffer still more for God.

He that loves God and suffers at the same time, gains twofold merit for heaven. St. Vincent de Paul says that to be without suffering in this world should be counted the greatest misfortune. St. Francis of Assisi, on the day he spent without suffering, feared that God had forgotten him. St. John Chrysostom writes that when God gives a man the grace to suffer He does him a greater favor than if He had conferred upon him the power to raise the dead, because in working miracles, man is made a debtor to God, but in permitting suffering, God makes himself debtor to man. He adds that if one, who suffers something for God, receives nothing in return but the grace to suffer for God, he has already a great recompense. For this reason he thought St. Paul received a greater grace when he was thrown into chains than when he was rapt into the third heaven.

WITH PATIENCE

"Patience hath a perfect work" (James 1:4). Which means that nothing pleases God more than to see a soul suffering *with patience* all the crosses He sends. Love makes the lover similar to the beloved. St. John saw all the saints "clothed with white robes, and palms in their hands" (Apoc. 7:9). The palm is the sign of martyrdom. But since not all the saints are martyrs, how is it that all are carrying palms? St. Gregory gives the answer: all the saints have really been martyrs, either by the sword or by patience. Hence he adds: "We too can become martyrs without the sword, if we practice patience."

The Lord said to St. Teresa: "Do you imagine, my daughter, that merit consists in enjoyment? No, it consists in suffering and in loving. Look at My own life, entirely filled with suffering. Believe Me, My daughter, to the soul My Father loves more, He sends the greater pains, and the greatness of the pains is proportionate to the greatness of His love. Look at My wounds; all that you suffer will never come near to what I suffered from them." Then St. Teresa adds for our encouragement: "God never sends a cross without sending at once a reward for carrying it."

St. Louis of France tried to free the Holy Land from the Turks. But they defeated him and took him prisoner. He afterward said: "I rejoice and thank God more for the patience He gave me during my imprisonment than if I had conquered the whole world." On the death of her husband, Elizabeth of Thuringia was driven into exile together with her son, where she was left homeless and abandoned by all. She went to a Franciscan monastery and had the monks sing a hymn of thanksgiving to God for having granted her the favor to suffer something for His love.

But whoever longs for a reward in the next world must learn to struggle and suffer. "If we suffer, we shall also reign" (2 Tim. 2:12). Without merit, no reward; and without patience, no merit. Some persons, when there is question of the goods of this world, try by all means possible to get possession of all they can; when there is question of eternal goods, they say: "Oh, any old corner in heaven is good enough for me!" The saints speak a different language. In this world they are satisfied with anything; indeed they often deliberately renounce what they already own, but they try to lay up treasures in heaven as much as they can. Which of the two shows more common sense?

PATIENCE AND PEACE

But even in this world, the man who suffers with the most patience enjoys the most peace. St. Philip Neri used to say that in this world there is no purgatory: there is either heaven or hell; he that suffers with patience enjoys heaven, he that does not, endures hell. And that is true; for, as St. Teresa writes, whoever reaches out and embraces the cross no longer feels its weight.

St. Francis de Sales on one occasion, finding himself overwhelmed with tribulations, said: "From the time I began to meet with so much treacherous opposition, I have enjoyed an indescribable peace; these sufferings give me assurance that my soul will soon rest firmly in God, and that indeed is my only ambition, my one desire."

A certain devout man used to say: "Take the sweet things of this life for bitter, and the bitter things for sweet, and you will always enjoy peace."

A priest told one of his penitents, who was in great tribulation, to write at the foot of the crucifix: "This is true love."

Not the suffering itself, but the will to suffer, is the surest sign that a soul really loves God. What greater satisfaction can we have, says St. Teresa, than to possess proof that we are pleasing God!

"The sight of Jesus nailed to the cross," said a holy person, "renders the cross itself so dear, that it seems to me I could not be happy without the cross; the love of Jesus Christ gives me strength to bear everything."

We know what Jesus himself recommends to the one who wishes to follow Him: "Let him take up his cross . . . and follow me" (Luke 9:23). But – take it up and carry it, not through necessity and with disgust, but humbly, patiently, lovingly.

What pleasure he gives to God who lovingly and patiently embraces the cross God sends him! St. Ignatius of Loyola used to say: "There is no wood better adapted to produce and preserve the love of God than the wood of the holy cross," – that is, to love God in the midst of trials.

One "Blessed be God," when things go wrong, is worth more than a thousand thanksgivings when all is well.

WHAT BENEFIT?

St. Francis de Sales used to say: "Those trials which come from God, or from men with the permission of God, are always more precious than those which proceed from our own will; for it is a general rule that, where there is less of our own choice, there is more pleasure for God and more profit for ourselves."

St. Teresa gives the same admonition: "We make more progress in one day with the contradictions that come from God or from our neighbor than in 10 years of sufferings that we have chosen ourselves."

Listen to what St. Chrysostom says of a soul that has given itself entirely to God: "Once a man has arrived at the perfect love of God, he feels as though he were alone on this earth. He pays no heed to glory or contempt, he walks unmoved through trials and sufferings, he loses all taste and appetite for the things of this world, and finding no support or rest in any earthly thing, he seeks untiringly his beloved, and so, whether working or eating, whether waking or sleeping, in all his activity, his only thought and desire is to find his beloved, because where his heart is, there is his treasure also."

PRAYER

Dearly beloved Jesus, my only treasure, on account of the offenses I have committed against You, I no longer deserve to be able to love You, but by Your own merits I beg You, make me worthy of Your pure love. I love You above all things, and I repent with my whole heart of having at one time driven You from my soul; but now I love You. I love You with my whole heart. I fear nothing but to find myself deprived of Your holy love.

The years of life that remain to me, I wish to spend in loving You and in giving You pleasure. My Jesus, my Love, help me! Help a sinner who wishes to love You and to be wholly Yours!

O Mary, my hope, your Son hears your prayers; pray to Him for me and obtain for me the grace of perfect love.

CHAPTER VI

LOVE IS ALWAYS KIND

Whoever loves God, loves those whom God loves. Whoever loves God always goes about seeking to help others, to comfort others. This is the lesson taught by St. Francis de Sales, the teacher and model of kindness: "Humble kindness is the virtue of virtues so strongly recommended to us by God; therefore we should practice it always and everywhere."

Kindness should be practiced in a special way toward the poor, for they, precisely because they are poor, are generally treated harshly. It should also be practiced in a special manner toward the sick, who are afflicted and more or less abandoned in their infirmity.

In a still more special way kindness should be practiced toward enemies. "Overcome evil with good" (Rom. 12:21). We must conquer ill-feeling toward us by love. Such was the conduct of the saints, and they succeeded in winning the affection of their most stubborn enemies.

"Nothing," says St. Francis de Sales, "gives such edification as loving kindness." And so the saint generally went about with a smile, his face beaming with the charity which showed itself in all his words and actions. St. Vincent de Paul said that he never knew a kinder man. He said, further, that Bishop de Sales seemed to him to be the express image of the loving kindness of Jesus Christ. Even in refusing what he could not in conscience grant, he did it with such kindness that the applicants, though unsuccessful in their requests, went away satisfied and well-disposed toward him. He was kind toward all, superiors, equals and inferiors. He was kind everywhere, in his home and on the streets, not like those who, as he himself used to say, are angels abroad but demons at home.

FOR THOSE IN AUTHORITY

Anyone who holds authority over others should be full of kindness toward his subjects. In imposing a task, he should request rather than command. St. Vincent de Paul used to say: "There is no surer way of securing obedience than kindness." St. Jane de Chantal once said: "I have tried many ways of governing, and I have found none better than the sweet and patient way."

Kindness should be shown even in corrections. We should sometimes give a strong reproof when the fault is great and when the fault has been repeated after due admonition; but we should take care never to reprove bitterly or angrily. Whoever reproves in this manner does more harm than good.

If ever, on some rare occasion, it should be needful to make a cutting remark in order to bring an offender to a sense of his guilt, we should never, even then, dismiss him without some kind word, so that he may go away with a good taste in his mouth.

"You know not what manner of spirit you are" (Luke 9:55). Thus spoke Jesus Christ to the disciples James and John when they wished to call down chastisements on the Samaritans who had driven them out of the country. "What spirit," He said, "is this? Surely it is not mine, which is kindness; for I have not come to destroy, but to save."

In fact, with what kindness Jesus treated the adulteress! "Woman," He said, "has no man condemned you? Neither will I condemn you. Go, and now sin no more" (John 8:10-11). He was satisfied with warning her not to sin again, and then He sent her away in peace. With what kindness He tried to convert, and indeed did convert, the Samaritan woman! First He asked her for a drink; then He said: "If you knew who he is that says to you, 'Give me to drink!' " Then He revealed to her that He was the expected Messiah. With what gentleness He sought to convert the traitor Judas, permitting him to share the food on His own plate, washing his feet, admonishing him in the very moment of his treacherous act: "Judas, do you betray me thus with a kiss?"

See how He converted Peter after Peter had denied Him. As He was leaving the house of the high priest, without a word of reproof, He gave Peter a look of tenderness and converted him — converted him so radically that never till his dying day did Peter cease to weep over the wrong he had done to his Master.

KINDNESS AND HARSHNESS

See how much more can be gained by kindness than by harshness.

St. Francis de Sales, by kindness, obtained whatever he sought; and he even succeeded in bringing back to God the most obstinate sinners.

When we must speak to somebody who has insulted us, we should take great care to be kind. But if we are excited, it is better to keep quiet, otherwise we shall think we are justified in saying whatever comes to our lips, and afterward, when we are calm again, we shall see that we did wrong.

When it happens that we ourselves commit a fault, we must be patient toward ourselves. To become exasperated with ourselves is not humility; it is a subtle pride; it is refusing to admit that we are weak creatures liable at any moment to fall into sin.

When we are upset we cannot clearly see our duty, and we find it difficult to do the will of God. After a fault we should turn at once to God with humility and confidence, beg His pardon and say, with St. Catherine of Genoa: "Look, Lord, these are the weeds that grow in my garden. I love You with my whole heart, and I am sorry I gave You this displeasure. I do not want to do it again. Help me."

PRAYER

My Jesus, I love You. I give myself entirely to You. Never, never again, beloved Lord, will I cease to love You. To atone for my sins, You allowed Yourself to be bound as a criminal, and so bound, to be led through the streets of Jerusalem to Your death. You have willed to be nailed to the cross and there to give up Your life. By the merits of so much suffering, never permit me to separate myself from You!

I repent of having, at one time, turned my back upon You, and I propose, by Your grace, rather to die than willfully offend You again.

O Mary, my hope, help me to be kind to all for love of your Son.

CHAPTER VII

LOVE IS NEVER ENVIOUS

Whoever loves Jesus Christ does not envy the great and famous persons of the world, but envies only those who love God more than he does.

St. Gregory explains this third sign of love. He that loves God cannot envy worldly greatness which he does not desire. Therefore we must distinguish two kinds of envy: the one wicked, the other holy.

Wicked envy is that which causes us to grieve because others enjoy earthly goods which we do not.

Holy envy is that which makes us rather pity the great ones of this world who live in the midst of worldly riches and pleasures. It makes us seek and desire God alone and strive after nothing but to love Him as much as we can, and therefore to look with holy envy on those who love Him more than we.

GOD'S GOOD PLEASURE

Some people, in their conduct, have unworthy motives: human respect, hankering after honors, quest of riches, or, if nothing else, self-satisfaction; but the saints have only one purpose in all they do, that is, God's good pleasure.

It is not sufficient that what we do is good; the way we do it must also be good. We must do it with the intention of pleasing God. This was the praise merited by Jesus Christ: "He did all things well" (Mark 7:37).

Many actions are praiseworthy in themselves, but because they are done for something else besides the glory of God, they are of little or no value in the sight of God.

One saint said: "God rewards our actions according to our singleness of purpose." But how difficult it is to find an action done solely for God!

A holy old monk had labored hard for God. One day, after a glance at his past life, he said: "How sad! When I examine all the actions of my life, I do not find a single one that was done for God alone!"

It is self-love which makes us lose all or at least the great part of the fruit of our good works.

Our Lord says: "Take heed that you do not your justice before men to be seen by them; otherwise you shall not have a reward of your Father who is in heaven" (Matt. 6:1).

The prophet Aggeus says that whoever works for anything else but the glory of God, puts his wages in a sack full of holes; when he opens the sack, he will find nothing there. Such a one, when he fails to attain the object he had in view, is terribly upset. And that is a clear proof that he was not working solely for the glory of God; because when a man does something solely for the glory of God, he is not disquieted even when the undertaking fails. He has already attained his purpose, which was to please God. God is pleased because the man worked with a pure intention.

GUIDELINES

Here are some signs or marks showing that one engaged in a spiritual undertaking is working solely for God: 1) He is not disturbed if the work fails. Since God does not will its success, neither does he. 2) He is quite as happy when others succeed as when he does so himself. 3) He does not desire one assignment rather than another, but cheerfully accepts what his superiors decide upon. 4) When he has finished his task he does not look for thanks or approval, and so if ever his work is criticized and belittled, he is not afflicted. God is pleased, and that is all he asks. If on the other hand the world applauds, he is not puffed up.

If we have the happy lot to be found worthy to do something that gives pleasure to God, what greater reward could we desire? This is the greatest reward, the greatest good fortune to which a creature could aspire, to be able to give pleasure to its Creator.

It has been said that the pure intention of acting only for the purpose of pleasing God is the heavenly alchemy that transforms iron into gold; that is, the most trivial actions, such as eating, working, playing, sleeping, when done for God, are changed into the gold of holy love.

TRUE INDIFFERENCE

The lovers of Jesus Christ acquire a total indifference; the sweet and the bitter are alike to them; they seek nothing for themselves but everything for God. They are equally content in outstanding or insignificant employments, in agreeable or repugnant tasks. If God is pleased, they are happy.

Many, on the contrary, wish to serve God, but only in this particular work, in this particular place, with these particular companions, under these particular circumstances; otherwise they abandon the work entirely or perform it reluctantly. Such persons lack the liberty of the children of God; they are slaves of self-love, and therefore they have little merit even in the good that they do and they live a disturbed life.

This means that we must be detached even from our prayers when Our Lord wants us to be at work.

One day, when a priest was overburdened with work, he was eager to rid himself of it all so he could go and pray; for it seemed to him that so much activity prevented him from remaining close to God. It was then the Lord said to him: "Even though I do not keep you here beside Me, be content that I send you to do My bidding."

Some persons worry because they are sometimes obliged by obedience or charity to omit some of their regular devotions. They can be sure that such worry does not come from God, but from the devil or from their own self-love.

Do what pleases God, then let come what may! That is the motto of the saints.

PRAYER

Eternal God, I offer You my whole heart. But what a sorry heart I have to offer! A heart created to love You, but, far from loving You, so often rebellious toward You! But look, my Jesus! If my poor heart was once rebellious now it is full of grief and repentance for the displeasure it has given You, and I am firmly resolved to obey You and love You. Draw me to Your love! Do it, I beg You, through the love You bore me while dying on the cross for me.

I love You, my Jesus; I love You with all my heart.

O Mary, my Mother, accept me as your servant, and beg Jesus, your Son, to receive me.

CHAPTER VIII

LOVE CHOOSES ONLY WHAT IS GOOD

According to St. Gregory charity or love of God cannot approve anything that is not right and just. The same thought is well expressed by the apostle St. Paul. Love, he says, is the bond binding together in the soul all the most perfect virtues. "But above all these things, have love, which is the bond of perfection" (Col. 3:14). Since love strives for holiness, it naturally recoils from that indifference with which some persons pretend to serve God at the serious risk of losing divine love, the grace of God, the soul — everything.

This indifference or coolness in the service of God is referred to as lukewarmness. Mark well however that there are two kinds of lukewarmness: the one unavoidable, the other avoidable.

Unavoidable lukewarmness is that from which the saints themselves are not exempt. It includes all the defects we commit without full consent, but merely through human frailty. For example: distractions in prayer, overwrought feelings, idle words, vain curiosity, showing off before others, too much attention to food and drink, lack of promptness in controlling sensual inclinations, and the like.

HUMAN WEAKNESS

We should of course avoid these defects as much as we can; but, on account of the weakness of our nature infected by sin, it is impossible to avoid them all. We should also repent of them because they displease God; but we should take care not to let them worry us. St. Francis de Sales wrote: "Worrisome thoughts come not from God, the Prince of Peace, but from the devil, from self-love or from our too high opinion of ourselves."

Such faults are indeed defects, but they do not hinder holiness, that is, they do not prevent us from walking on the road to holiness; for nobody in this world actually reaches perfect holiness until he arrives at the kingdom of the blessed.

The lukewarmness, however, that really does hinder perfection is *avoidable* lukewarmness, by which one commits deliberate venial sins; for all these faults committed with open eyes can be avoided with the grace of God.

St. Teresa used to say: "From deliberate sin, no matter how little it may be, the Lord deliver you!" Such are, for example: little lies, backbiting, ridiculing others, angry and cutting remarks, boasting, spitefulness.

A holy priest said that during his life he had committed innumerable faults, but that he had never made peace with them. Some persons make peace with their faults, and this brings about their ruin, especially if the fault proceeds from self-love, thirst for popularity, money-grabbing, spitefulness in regard to a certain person, or from inordinate affection for somebody of the opposite sex. For such persons there is great danger.

THE LITTLE "LIKES"

Many spiritual persons fall short of holiness because they will not renounce certain little attachments.

All the harm comes from the feeble love they have for Jesus Christ. Some are bloated with self-esteem. Some lose heart when things do not go according to their wishes. Some baby themselves on the plea of delicate health. Some keep their heart wide open to external attractions and their mind full of distractions by their eagerness to hear and learn so many things that have nothing to do with the service of God but merely cater to idle curiosity. Some are filled with resentment at every trifling lack of attention which they imagine they have suffered and allow themselves to grow so disturbed as to neglect prayer. Some are all piety and sweetness one day, all gloom and peevishness the next, accordingly as daily happenings agree or disagree with their whims. None of these really love Jesus Christ, or they love Him very little, and they bring discredit on true devotion.

The helps that can be used by anyone to avoid or overcome indifference or lukewarmness in the loving service of God are: the desire for holiness; the determination to succeed; meditation; frequent Communion; prayer.

THE DESIRE FOR HOLINESS

Holy desires, says St. Lawrence Justinian, increase our strength and lessen our pain. They give us the force to march ahead on the road to holiness, and they lighten the difficulties along the way. Whoever has this genuine desire never stops on the road to holiness. And he who never stops, finally arrives. On the contrary, whoever has not this desire, will always go backward and find himself ever more guilty of faults than before.

It is a great mistake to say: "God does not expect us all to be holy." St. Paul says the contrary: "This is . . . the will of God, your sanctification" (1 Thess. 4:3).

God *does* want everybody to be holy — each in his own state: the religious as a religious, lay people as lay people, the priest as a priest, the married man as a married man, the merchant as a merchant, the soldier as a soldier, and the same for every other state in life.

Of marvelous beauty are the admonitions which St. Teresa gives on this subject. In one place she says: "Let our ideals be high; that is the secret of true progress." In another place she says: "Never lose heart, but trust in God, for by manly efforts we can, little by little, with the help of God, reach the heights which the saints have reached before us."

In another place she says: "God does not give many great graces except to those who have a great desire for His love." In yet another place she says: "God is not slow in repaying, even in this life, every good desire, for He loves generous souls, provided they do not proudly presume on their own strength."

Courage then! Great courage! "The Lord is good . . . to the soul that seeks Him." God is good and generous to every soul that seeks Him in earnest. Neither can our past sins hinder us from becoming holy if we really want to. St. Teresa declares: "The devil tries to make us think it is pride to have lofty desires and to wish to imitate the saints; but it is really a great help thus to arouse ourselves for noble efforts because, even though we are not yet strong enough to go the whole way, we shall surely make great progress."

St. Paul writes: "To them that love God all things work together unto good" (Romans 8:28). Even past sins can help us to become holy, insofar as the thought of them makes us more humble and more thankful because of God's goodness toward us after we have offended Him.

If we have good desires, let us take heart and, trusting in God's help, set to work to put them into practice. If we meet with obstacles on the way, let us be calm and conform ourselves to the divine will. God's will must be preferred even to our good desires.

THE DETERMINATION TO SUCCEED

The second step which we must take in order to advance toward God with fervor and devotion is to make up our minds to do so. Many persons are called to holiness, urged to holiness and desire holiness, but because they never really make up their mind to get down to work to acquire holiness, they live and die in mediocrity.

The desire of holiness is not enough without the resolution to follow through. There are many who feed their soul on empty desires, but they never take one step on the road to God. It is of such desires the Scriptures speak: "Desires kill the slothful" (Prov. 21:25). The lazy person is always desiring, but never does he take the means, proper to his state in life, to become holy.

In the meantime he cannot put up with a neighbor, he cannot bear a word of contradiction, he fills his mind with a thousand useless cares, he commits numberless faults of curiosity and pride; and then he sighs: "Oh, if I could! Oh, if I had! Oh, if this! Oh, if that!"

St. Francis de Sales says: "I can never stand to see a person, who already has his duty or his vocation, always hankering after pious practices that are incompatible with his duty or his vocation; he merely dissipates his energies and grows lax in the performance of practices he could and should be attending to."

We should desire holiness and resolutely use the means to acquire it.

This is where meditation helps. During meditation we find the means leading to holiness. There are those who make meditation often, but never arrive at any solid resolution. St. Teresa says: "I prefer meditation that has been practiced for only a short time rather than meditation through many years wherein the soul never does reach the point of making a resolution to do something worthwhile for God." In another place she says: "I know from experience that if, at the beginning, one resolves to do something solely for God, no matter how difficult it may be, he need not fear failure."

Our first resolution should be to make every effort not to commit another deliberate sin, no matter how small. It is true that, without divine help, all our efforts will not suffice to overcome temptations, but if we are ready to do, at all times, what lies in our power, God, with His grace, will come to the aid of our weakness and lead us to victory.

This resolution to avoid deliberate sin removes all obstacles from our path and gives us great courage by assuring us that we are in sanctifying grace. St. Francis de Sales writes: "The greatest certitude we can have in this world of being in the grace of God consists, not in any feeling of love, but in the simple and irrevocable abandonment of ourselves into His hands and in the firm resolution never to consent to any sin, whether great or small."

St. Lawrence Justinian writes: "When one is really walking on the road to holiness, he feels an interior eagerness to make progress; and the more he advances, the greater does that eagerness become, because with the daily increasing divine light, he sees his helplessness so clearly that it seems to him he has no virtue and does nothing good, or, if he does discover some good, it seems to him so insignificant that he makes little account of it; and so he constantly strives really to grow in holiness without ever wearying."

We must do it *now* — not put it off until tomorrow. Who can assure us that we shall have tomorrow? "Whatsoever your hand is able to do, do it earnestly" (Eccl. 9:10). David wrote: "And I said, now I have begun" (Ps. 76:2). St. Charles Borromeo constantly repeated the same: "Today I begin to serve God in earnest." So we too must work each day as though until now we had done no good at all.

The saints know no miserliness when there is question of pleasing God who has given us all without reserve. St. Chrysostom writes: "He gave everything to you; He kept nothing for himself." God gave you himself, totally, entirely; and will you go haggling about how much you will give Him? "Christ died for all, that they also who live may not now live to themselves, but unto Him who died for them" (2 Cor. 5:15).

MEDITATION

The third means for advancing on the road to holiness is meditation.

The truths of faith are not seen with the eyes of the body; they are seen with the eyes of the mind, when it turns to reflection, to meditation. Whoever does not meditate does not see these truths, and therefore he walks in darkness, and in this obscurity it easily happens that he attaches himself to sensible objects and for their sake rejects those that are eternal.

St. Teresa said: "It may well happen that we imagine we find no imperfections in ourselves, but when God opens our eyes, as He is wont to do in meditation, we can see plenty."

St. Teresa also said: "If one perseveres in meditation, I hold for certain that, no matter how many times the devil may lead him astray, Our Lord will finally guide him into the harbor of salvation." Again she says: "Whoever does not wander from the path of meditation will arrive; late perhaps, but he will arrive."

What precious fruits we gather from meditation! There we conceive holy thoughts, we converse lovingly with God, we stir up generous desires, we make strong resolutions to give ourselves entirely to God; and so we learn to sacrifice worldly pleasures and all inordinate inclinations.

Nobody should make meditation in order to feel the sweetness of divine love; whoever does this will waste his time or gather scanty fruit. He should meditate solely in order to please God, that is, solely to learn what God wants him to do and to beg of God the strength to do it.

He that does not meditate will not pray. In my spiritual books I have often spoken of the necessity of prayer, and particularly in a booklet entitled, "On Prayer, the Great Means of Salvation." Here I will touch on the question briefly. It will be sufficient to cite the words of a holy bishop: "How can we remain in sanctifying grace if God does not give us perseverance? How can we expect Him to give us perseverance if we do not ask for it? And how will we ask for it if we do not meditate? If we do not meditate we shall not go to God for strength to live right."

Whoever does not meditate scarcely sees the needs of his soul, scarcely recognizes the dangers to his salvation, scarcely knows the means he should use to conquer temptations.

Whoever loves Jesus Christ and desires to grow in His love, will find no subject for meditation more efficacious than the passion of our Redeemer.

St. Francis de Sales calls the Mount of Calvary the Mount of Lovers. At the sight of a God, dying because He loves us, dying to make us love Him, it is impossible not to love Him ardently.

FREQUENT COMMUNION

The fourth means that can help us to overcome indifference in our spiritual life and to make great progress on the road toward God is frequent Communion.

St. Teresa says: "There is no greater aid to holiness than frequent Communion. How marvelously the Lord shows His power therein!"

St. John Chrysostom says that Communion makes us eager for virtue and prompt to practice it, at the same time imparting deep peace, and thus rendering sweet and easy the road to holiness.

Although it is most expedient that they who communicate frequently or daily should be free from venial sins, at least from such as are fully deliberate, and from all affection thereto, nevertheless it is sufficient that they be free from serious sin, with the firm purpose of never sinning mortally in the future; and, if they have this firm purpose, daily communicants will gradually free themselves from even venial sins, and from all affection thereto.

Further, to derive rich fruit from Communion a devout thanksgiving is necessary. The time after Communion can be made rich in graces for us if we give sufficient time to it. The time after Communion is the time to amass treasures of grace. St. Teresa writes: "After Communion let us take care not to lose such a profitable occasion of striking a bargain with God; His Divine Majesty is not accustomed to give niggardly pay for the lodgings where He has received generous hospitality."

In order to preserve the soul in fervor another great help is *spiritual Communion. Spiritual* Communion, as St. Thomas explains, consists in an ardent desire to receive Jesus Christ in the Blessed Sacrament. That is why the saints were accustomed to make it many times a day. This is the way to make a spiritual Communion: "My Jesus, I believe that You are present in the Blessed Sacrament. I love You, and I desire You. Come into my soul. I welcome You, and

I beg You never to permit me to separate myself from You." A shorter form: "My Jesus, come to me; I desire You, I welcome You. Keep me always united with You."

This spiritual Communion can be made many times a day: during meditation, during the visit to the Blessed Sacrament, and at any time of the day no matter where you are.

PRAYER

The fifth and most necessary means for rising above indifference and truly advancing on the road to holiness is prayer.

And let me say, first of all, that in giving us this great means of prayer God shows us how much He loves us. What stronger proof of affection could anyone give to his friend than to say to him: "My friend, ask from me whatever you wish, and it is yours?" Now this is exactly what Our Lord says to us: "Ask, and it shall be given you; seek, and you shall find" (Luke 11:9).

Prayer is called omnipotent – it can obtain anything from God. He that prays obtains from God all he wants.

If we are poor in the possession of virtue, we can blame nobody but ourselves; we are poor because we want to be poor, and therefore we deserve no pity. Look at our God, says St. Paul, ready to enrich everybody who appeals to Him.. "Rich unto all that call upon Him" (Romans 10:12).

Humble prayer is useful to obtain everything from God; but we should know that, besides being useful, prayer is necessary for salvation. It is certain that we have absolute need of God's help to resist temptations; and, sometimes the ordinary help which God gives to everybody should suffice, but in fact, on account of our evil inclinations, it will not suffice, and extraordinary help will be needed. He who prays will receive that help.

The holy writers say that prayer is necessary for us, not only *by necessity of precept* but also *by necessity of means,* that is, a necessity so absolute that whoever does not pray simply cannot be saved. The reason, briefly, is that we cannot save our soul without the help of divine grace, and God does not give this grace unless we pray. Because our temptations and our dangers of falling into sin are continual, continual also must be our prayer.

St. Thomas says: "Unceasing prayer is necessary for entrance into heaven." And before him Jesus Christ said: "We ought always to pray and not to faint" (Luke 18:1).

Though it is true that we cannot really merit perseverance, nevertheless St. Augustine says that in a certain broad sense we can merit it. "This gift of God, called perseverance, can be supplicatingly merited, that is, it can be secured by supplication." The Lord wants to give us His graces, but He wants to be asked.

We should have unbounded confidence in prayer. God has pledged himself to hear us when we pray. "Ask, and you shall receive" (John 16:24). How can we doubt, says St. Augustine, since by making this promise God has obliged himself to grant us the graces for which we ask? Whenever we recommend ourselves to God, we must have the certain confidence that He will hear us, and we shall obtain everything we want. He himself says: "All things whatsoever you ask when you pray, believe that you shall receive, and they shall come unto you" (Mark 11:24).

But I am a sinner; I do not deserve to be heard. Remember that Jesus Christ says: "Everyone who asks receives." *Everyone* be he just or sinner. St. Thomas says: "The power of our prayers to obtain

God's help comes not from our merits, but from the divine mercy."

In order to take away all fear of not being heard when we pray, our Savior says: "Amen, amen, I say unto you, if you shall ask the Father anything in my name, he will give it to you" (John 16:23). These words can be understood to mean: "Sinner, you do not deserve to receive favors through your own merits; therefore do thus: when you want a favor, supplicate My Father in My name, that is, by *My merits and My love.* Then ask whatever you please, and you will get it."

When we ask for temporal favors, we should always ask on condition that they are useful for our eternal salvation; but when we ask for spiritual favors, we should ask without any condition, but with certain confidence of being heard, saying: "Eternal Father, in the name of Jesus Christ, free me from this temptation, grant me holy perseverance, give me Your love, bring me to paradise." We can ask these favors also of Jesus Christ in His own name, that is, through His merits, because here too, we have His promise: "If you ask me anything in my name, I will do it" (John 14:14).

When we ask God for His favors, let us not forget to recommend ourselves also to Mary, the dispenser of God's graces. St. Bernard says it is God indeed who gives the favor, but He gives it through the hands of Mary. "Let us ask favors and ask them through Mary, because what she asks she receives, and she cannot be refused."

PRAYER

Jesus, my Love, I am firmly determined to love You as much as I can and to become holy. And the reason I am determined to become holy is to give You pleasure and to love You in this life and in the next. I myself can do nothing, but You can do everything; and I know that You wish me to be holy. I wish to live no longer for myself. You desire me to be wholly Yours, and wholly Yours I desire to be. You are my hope, my love, my all!

I will not lose heart about becoming holy on account of the offenses I have committed against You in past years; I know, my Jesus, that You have died to pardon those who repent. I love You now with my whole soul; I love You with my whole heart. I love You more than myself, and I repent above all else of having despised You, My loving God. Give me help, give me strength, during the days of life that yet remain, to make amends, by my love, for the many times I have failed during the past.

Queen of heaven, Mother of God, advocate of sinners, I trust in you!

CHAPTER IX

LOVE IS NEVER BOASTFUL OR CONCEITED

A person who truly loves Jesus Christ does not have a high opinion of his own excellence.

He who loves God is truly humble. He does not become puffed up on seeing something praiseworthy in himself; for he knows that whatever he has is a gift of God and that all he can claim as his own is sin. When he sees all that God has done for him, he humbles himself the more, acknowledging that he is unworthy to be so greatly favored by God.

St. Teresa, speaking of the special favors God had given her, says: "God supports me just as we prop up an old house to keep it from falling to pieces."

Whenever we see ourselves especially favored by God, precisely then we should humble ourselves the more. Every time St. Teresa received some special favor she recalled to mind all the faults she had committed, and because of her humility the Lord united himself more intimately with her. The more a soul acknowledges itself unworthy of favors, the more God enriches it with favors.

We read of St. Margaret of Cortona that one day, when Our Lord visited her with greater loving tenderness than usual, she exclaimed: "But, Lord, have You forgotten what I used to be? Do you repay me with such sweetness for the sins I have committed?" And God replied that, when a soul loves Him and sincerely repents of having offended Him, He forgets all the offenses — just as the prophet Ezechiel writes: "But if the wicked do penance . . . I will not remember all his iniquities" (18:21-22). If we could only comprehend the value of humility! A single act of humility is worth more than all the riches of the world.

STRENGTH FOR ALL THINGS

The proud person trusts in his own strength, and so he falls; but the humble man, because he trusts only in God, even though assaulted by all the most violent temptations, stands firm, and does not fall. His motto is: "I can do all things in him who strengthens me" (Phil. 4:13).

The Imitation notes several cases in which our humility will be put to the test. "What others say shall be heeded; what you say shall be deemed trivial; you shall ask and be repulsed. Others shall be loudly praised by men; you shall be passed over in silence. To others shall be committed this office and that; but you shall be judged fit for nothing. In these and like things is the Lord wont to try His faithful servant, to show in how far he is able to deny and overcome himself. Nature shall at times be saddened, but you shall have great gain if you bear all in silence."

Some people are like porcupines: they seem so gentle and placid, so long as they are not touched; but when someone admonishes them about a failing, they instantly become covered with bristling quills. They retort bitterly that the charge is untrue, or that they were right in acting as they did, and that they cannot understand why they should be blamed. In a word, whoever gives them a kindly admonition becomes their enemy — like the sick man who gets angry with the surgeon for treating his painful wounds. The holy and humble man, says St. John Chrysostom, when he is corrected, grieves for the fault committed; the proud man too grieves when corrected, but he grieves because his fault has been uncovered, and so he is upset and gives an angry retort to the one that admonished him.

Here is the beautiful rule St. Philip Neri tells us to follow when we are reprimanded: "Whoever honestly wishes to become holy should never excuse himself, even though the accusation be false." The sole exception would be when there would be danger of scandal. What rich merit he acquires in the sight of God who, when blamed, even unjustly, keeps silent and does not excuse himself! St. Teresa says: "Sometimes a person makes more progress in holiness by refraining from excusing himself than by listening to 10 sermons, for by overcoming the inclination to excuse himself he really begins to possess liberty of spirit and to be indifferent whether others speak well or ill of him."

LOVE IS NOT AMBITIOUS

Whoever loves Jesus Christ does not look for the esteem and love of men; his only desire is to be pleasing to God, who is the only object of his love.

St. James writes: "God resists the proud and gives His grace to the humble" (James 4:6). "Resists the proud," that is, He does not even listen to their prayers; and among the acts of pride surely this is one: to go looking for popularity and to be conceited when you gain it.

When we hear of the fall of certain persons who were considered very devout, we may surmise that they did not give themselves entirely to God, but that they had cherished a secret pride which led to their downfall. How we should tremble when we discover within ourselves a certain ambition to appear before the world and win its applause. If ever the world does applaud us, let us guard well against any vain complacency, for it could cause a lot of trouble for us.

Let us particularly guard against touchiness on points of honor. St. Teresa says where there is that kind of touchiness there can be little love of God. There are many who profess to live a holy life, while in reality they are self-idolaters. They exhibit certain external virtues, but they want to be praised for them. If nobody else praises them, they praise themselves. They want to have the reputation of being better than others. Not so the true lovers of God. Never do they say a word in their own praise or seek the praise of others.

The saying of St. Francis of Assisi is only too true: "I am what I am in the sight of God." What does it profit us to stand high in the opinion of the world if before God we are unacceptable? On the other hand what does it matter to be ignored by the world if we are dear and pleasing in the eyes of God?

A bad conscience is not healed by flattery nor a good conscience wounded by gossip. He that praises us cannot take away the punishment we deserve for our evil deeds, neither can he that reviles us deprive us of the reward of our good works.

How safe is a hidden life for those who would love Jesus Christ! Jesus himself has given us the example of living hidden for 30 years in a workshop. That is why the saints, in order to evade human praise, have gone to spend their lives in deserts and in caves. The desire to attract attention, says St. Vincent de Paul, to have others speak well of us, praise our way of acting, say that we succeed — this, he says, is a fault which, making us forget God, vitiates our holiest actions and blocks all progress in the spiritual life.

Whoever therefore honestly desires to advance in the love of Jesus Christ must overcome his vanity by being willing to remain hidden and unknown to others.

PRAYER

My Jesus, give me the desire to please You and to forget all creatures, even myself. What does it profit me to be loved by all the world, if I am not loved by You? My Jesus, You came into this world to gain our hearts. If I do not know how to give You my heart, then take it, fill it with Your love, and never permit it again to be separated from You. In the past I have turned my back on You, but now, seeing the evil I have done, I repent with my whole heart. Nothing pains me more than the remembrance of the many offenses I have committed against You. My consolation is in the knowledge that You are infinite goodness and that You do not refuse to love a sinner who loves You.

My cherished Redeemer, in the past I have despised You, but now I love You more than myself. I have no other desire than to love You and to give You pleasure. This is my ambition. Accept it, strengthen it, and extinguish in me all desires for worldly things. You are exceedingly worthy of love, and You have gone to great lengths to win my love.

I trust also in you, Mary, O great Mother of God. Help me!

CHAPTER X

LOVE CAN SACRIFICE

Whoever desires to love Jesus Christ with his whole heart must necessarily keep his heart free from everything that might prevent him from giving himself completely to God. First on the list of things to be surrendered is self-love. Unselfish love tries to learn what is God's pleasure and prefers God's pleasure to its own.

That is what God demands of us when He says: "You shall love the Lord, your God, with your whole heart."

To love God with your whole heart, you must do two things: clear your heart of all the things of earth; fill your heart with the love of God.

The heart in which there remains an earthly affection can never belong entirely to God. St. Philip Neri says that the more love for creatures we put into our heart, the less room we leave for the love of God.

But how can we empty our heart of the things of earth? By mortification and by detachment from created things. Many persons complain that they seek God and cannot find Him. St. Teresa tells them what to do: "Separate your heart from creatures; then seek God, and you will find Him."

Many persons deceive themselves when they aspire to close friendship with God, because they follow their own method; they wish to love Jesus Christ, but with their own peculiar brand of love, without giving up too worldly amusements, vanity in dress, lack of moderation in eating and drinking. They say they love God; but if they do not succeed in securing a status to which they aspire, they are agitated and unhappy; if their reputation is touched, they fly into a rage; if they are not cured of some bodily ailment, they lose patience. They say they love God; but they do not give up their love of wealth or their yearning for worldly honors, or the desire of wanting to be considered wiser or better than others. They pray, they go to Communion; but, because their heart is filled with the things of earth, they carry away little benefit.

A NOISY WORLD

To such as these the Lord does not even speak; He sees it would be a waste of time. That is what He said one day to St. Teresa: "There are many to whom I long to speak, but the world makes such a noise in their ears that they cannot hear Me. If they would only detach themselves a little from the world!"

Whoever is filled with worldly affections cannot even hear God's voice when God does speak to him. Unhappy the man who is attached to the things of this world. For the day may come — and all too quickly — when, blinded by his infatuation for them, he will cease to love Jesus Christ, and, in order not to lose these passing goods, he may lose God, the eternal good.

God wills that He, and He alone, should be adored and loved by us, because it is His due, and because He has such love for us. Because He loves us so much, He wants all our love, and therefore He is jealous of anybody that takes away a part of those hearts which He wants entirely for himself.

Jesus is a jealous lover, says St. Jerome, and therefore He does not want us to give our love to anybody but himself. If ever He sees that some creature has part of our heart, He is, in a certain sense, jealous of that creature, as St. James writes, for He wants to be loved alone and without rivals. "Or do you think that the Scripture says in vain: the Spirit which dwells in you covets unto jealousy?" (James 4:5)

St. John of the Cross says: "The soul whose affections remain attached to anything whatever, no matter how small, in spite of all the virtues it practices, will never attain to the divine union; for it makes little difference whether a thread or a rope holds the bird captive; it is bound, and it cannot fly." He continues, "How pitiful it is to see certain souls, rich in pious practices, in virtues and in divine favors, who, for lack of courage to finish once and for all with some foolish little affection, remain incapable of attaining to divine union! While to attain to that union nothing more is necessary than one strong effort to break that thread; for, once a soul is emptied of earth, it is impossible that God should not come and communicate to it His own fullness."

Whoever wishes that God should be wholly his, must give himself wholly to God. Jesus Christ, for the great love He bears us, wants all our love, and so long as He does not have it, He is never content.

We must therefore pray God to purge our heart from all attachment to earth. "Create a clean heart in me, O God" (Psalm 50:12). He has made it clear to us that whoever does not renounce the things of earth cannot be His disciple. "Every one of you that does not renounce all that he possesses, cannot be my disciple" (Luke 14:33).

When a heart is emptied of created things, divine love at once enters and fills it. St. Teresa says: "Remove from your sight the attractions of the world; at once your soul will turn to the love of God." For the soul cannot live without loving. It must necessarily love: either Creator or creatures.

Our heart is so small! And shall we still try to divide this heart between creatures and God?

ONE GREAT PURPOSE

In the present life this should be for us the only thought, the only purpose: to seek God in order to love Him; to strive to learn His holy will in order to fulfill it. Happy the man who can say: "My Jesus, for love of You I have renounced all things. You are my only love. You alone are sufficient for me."

The moment divine love takes full possession of a soul, that soul, of its own initiative (presupposing, of course, the help of divine grace), sets to work to strip itself of every worldly thing that could hinder its belonging entirely to God.

St. Francis de Sales writes: "The pure love of God burns up everything that is not God in order to turn everything into itself, for all that is done for the love of God *is* the love of God."

A person who wishes to love God truly must always be on his guard against vainglory. Many souls, on account of the desire to stand high in the opinion of others and to make an impression on the people around them, never come really close to God in their love for Him because of surrendering to this insidious inclination to vainglory. If, for example, they are accused of a fault, what efforts they make to justify themselves and to prove that the accusation is nothing but lies and calumny! If they happen to do something good and commendable, what efforts they make to let it be known to all the world – at least to the little world around them! They want everybody to know about their accomplishments so that praise will be offered from all sides.

How different is the conduct of the saints! The saints were happy if everybody knew their faults, so that everybody would consider them the unworthy and sinful persons they honestly believed themselves to be. If the saints performed acts even of great virtue, they wanted it to be known only to God, whom alone they were trying to please. The saints desired to be hidden and unknown, mindful of the words of Jesus Christ: "When you give alms, let not your left hand know what your right hand does" (Matt. 6:3). And also: "When you pray, go into your room and shut the door; then pray to your Father in secret" (Matt. 6:6).

SELF-WILL

Union with God requires above all detachment from self-will.

Whoever knows how to conquer himself will easily conquer all difficulties that he meets. "Conquer yourself!" This was the slogan which St. Francis Xavier used to give to everybody.

Jesus Christ said: "If any man wishes to follow me, let him deny himself" (Matt. 16:24). In those few words we have the secret of all we need to do in order to sanctify ourselves: deny our *self* and our self-will. To be able to do this, says St. Francis of Assisi, is the greatest gift we can receive from God — to overcome ourselves by renouncing our self-will.

Unhappy the man who lives a slave to his own will! He will want many things that he cannot have, and he will be obliged to put up with many things he does not want or like.

The first battle we have to fight begins because of disturbance in our inclinations toward sensual satisfactions. Get away from the things that arouse your inclinations, guard your eyes, recommend yourself to God, and the battle will be over or at least the victory will be easy.

Another kind of struggle arises from our natural desire for wealth. Learn to live in the spirit of poverty, and the war will stop.

A third kind of war we have to fight over and over results from our hankering after honors. Learn to love humility and a quiet, hidden life, and the war will be over.

A fourth and most disastrous war is declared against us by our self-will — the powerful desire to have our own way in all things. If we strive to be resigned in all things to the will of God, victory will be ours.

GOD'S WILL

Many spiritual persons would like to attain to union with God, but without accepting the crosses God sends them. They are not resigned to an illness with which they are afflicted, they are passively rebellious against the poverty they cannot escape, they will not endure with patience the insults they receive; but without this resignation they will never reach perfect union with God.

Listen to the suggestion of St. Catherine of Genoa: "In order to arrive at union with God it is necessary to accept the adversity which He sends in order to consume all our evil inclinations, whether interior or exterior. Until we reach the point where adversity no longer seems bitter but sweet for God's dear sake, we shall never attain to the divine union."

What does it mean to give one's self entirely to God? It means: avoiding everything that is displeasing to God and doing what is pleasing to Him; it means accepting wholeheartedly everything that comes from God's hands, however difficult or disagreeable it may be; it means preferring in everything God's will to our own will.

PRAYER

In spite of my ingratitude and neglect in the past, O my God, I cannot help feeling that You are still inviting me, asking me to love You. I want to love You. I will resist no longer. I will no longer live for myself. You have done so much to deserve my love. I love You, Jesus, and I long for You. How could I love anyone or anything else but You after seeing You die in anguish on a cross to redeem me? How can I look at Your dead body, wasted with pain, and not love You with all my heart? Yes, my dear Redeemer, I do love You with my whole soul, and I desire to love only You during life and for all eternity.

My love, my hope, my strength, my consolation! Give me the grace to be faithful to You. Give me light to see the things from which I should detach myself, and give me strength to obey You in everything.

Give me the grace to think of nothing but You, to desire nothing but You, to seek nothing but You, my love and my only good!

Mary, Mother of God, obtain for me holy perseverance.

CHAPTER XI

LOVE IS NOT RESENTFUL

A person who truly loves God does not become impatient with his fellow human beings.

The virtue of patience, by which we restrain our anger and control our temper in trials, sufferings, contradictions, is a daughter of the virtue of meekness.

We have discussed meekness in previous chapters; but since everyone living in daily contact and association with others is continually called upon to practice and cultivate meekness, we shall discuss this virtue in some practical points.

Humility and meekness were virtues dear to Jesus Christ; therefore He made a special point of telling His disciples to learn to practice these virtues as He practiced them. "Learn of me, for I am meek and humble of heart" (Matt. 11:29). Our Redeemer was called a lamb. "Behold the Lamb of God" (John 1:29). This title belonged to Him since He would sacrifice himself as a lamb upon the cross to satisfy for our sins and also since He practiced meekness throughout His life, especially during His sufferings. In the house of Caiphas, one of the servants struck Him, on the pretense that He had answered the high priest with rash boldness, and asked: "Is this the way to give an answer to the high priest?" Jesus meekly replied: "If I have spoken evil, give testimony of the evil; but if I have spoken well, why do you strike me?" (John 18:23)

Jesus Christ continued to practice this virtue of meekness until the moment of His death. Hanging on the cross, He heard the men around Him mocking and blaspheming Him. His answer was a prayer to His eternal Father to forgive them. "Father, forgive them, for they do not know what they are doing" (Luke 23:34).

How Jesus must love the persons who, when they are insulted or laughed at, or calumniated, schemed against, persecuted and made to suffer pain in soul or body, are not provoked to anger against those who torment them! "The prayer of the meek is always pleasing to you" (Judith 9:16). This means that God always hears the prayers of those who practice meekness. To the meek the Lord has given a special promise of paradise. "Blessed are the meek, for they shall possess the land" (Matt. 5:4).

PEACE OF HEART

St. Francis de Sales said: "What is the whole world in comparison with peace of heart?" Indeed, of what use are all the riches, all the honors of the world to him who is constantly disturbed and deprived of peace of heart?

In order to remain always united to Jesus Christ we must do everything calmly without allowing ourselves to grow disturbed over the contradictions we meet with. "The Lord is not in the earthquake" (3 Kings 19:11). The Lord does not abide in agitated hearts.

Let us listen to the beautiful instructions of that master of meekness, St. Francis de Sales. "Let us never yield to anger, never open the door to anger under any pretext whatever, because once we have given entrance to anger we are no longer in a position to expel it or control it as we wish. If you want to conquer anger, follow these rules: reject it immediately by turning your mind to other matters, in the meantime taking care not to say even one impatient word. Like the apostles in the storm on Lake Genesareth, cry out at once to God to quiet the tempest in your heart. If ever your weakness allows you to fall into a temper, make every effort to regain your calmness, and then perform acts of humility and kindness toward the person against whom your anger has been aroused. All this must be done calmly and naturally, for it is highly important not to reopen the wounds."

Regarding this problem the saint said that during his life he had to fight hard against his two predominant passions: inordinate anger and inordinate love. He said it took him many long years of struggle to overcome his inclination to inordinate anger. As for inordinate love, he tried to change the object, by giving up creatures and directing all his affections to God. In this way he acquired such true and deep interior peace that it showed even exteriorly; and he was seen almost always with a serene countenance and a smile on his lips.

Whenever we feel provoked to anger by some disturbing incident, we imagine that, by giving way to it in deeds or at least in words, we shall experience relief and calm; but we deceive ourselves. We shall find that, after having given way to our anger, we shall be more agitated than before.

Whoever wishes to preserve continual peace of heart, must take care never to let himself get into a bad humor; and should he find that he is in a bad humor, he should see that he gets out of it at once, preventing it from spending the night with him. Let him try reading a book, or visiting a friend and conversing on pleasing topics.

PEACE IN GOD'S WILL

Anger lingers long in proud hearts which have little room for the love of Jesus Christ. But if by surprise anger gains entrance into a heart that loves Jesus Christ, it does not stay for long; it is promptly expelled. Whoever loves Jesus Christ with his whole heart never allows himself to be wrapped up in an angry mood. Conformity to the divine will renders him serene in every misfortune, and so he is equally kind to all. This persevering kindness, however, is never acquired without a great love for Jesus Christ. In fact, we find that we are never more meek and kind toward others than when we allow our affections to center in the heart of Christ.

Since it is not a simple matter to persevere at every moment in this devoted affection for Our Lord, we must prepare ourselves during mental prayer for all possible contradictions. Such was the method used by the saints; and they were always ready to receive with patience and meekness all slights and insults, even blows and bodily injury. The moment we are insulted, we shall, unless we have often prepared ourselves for such an event, find it extremely difficult to decide what we should do and what we should avoid in order not to be provoked to anger. In the surprise of the moment we may feel justified in resenting with indignation the insult we have not deserved.

DO NOT SPEAK IN ANGER

St. John Chrysostom says that by the fire of an angry answer we shall not extinguish the fire in the heart of our brother, but fan it into fiercer flame. "Fire is not put out by fire."

But is it reasonable to show courtesy and meekness toward some person who insults me for no cause at all? St. Francis de Sales says: "We must practice meekness not only when it is reasonable, but also when it is unreasonable." We must try to answer with a gentle word. That is the way to put out the fire. "A gentle answer is a quarrel averted" (Prov. 15:1). So long as our feelings are disturbed, the wiser course is to keep silence.

St. Bernard writes: "The eye that is clouded by anger sees nothing clearly." Vision obscured by resentment no longer distinguishes what is fair and what is unfair. We should make the same agreement with our tongue which St. Francis de Sales made with his. "I have made a pact with my tongue not to speak while my heart is disturbed."

It is sometimes lawful to be angry, provided we avoid any fault in our anger. But that is precisely the point. Speculatively speaking, it sometimes seems expedient to speak or to answer sharply in order to make another realize his fault; but in practice it is very difficult to do so without falling into some fault ourselves. Therefore the safest way is to admonish or answer always with kindness and never yield to resentment.

St. Francis de Sales said that he had never been provoked to anger, even in a good cause, without afterward regretting it. Therefore on such occasions, so long as we still feel upset and irritated, the safest way is to keep quiet and to postpone the admonition or the answer to a more opportune time when our temper has cooled.

WHEN BLAMED

We should make special efforts to practice this meekness when we are corrected or blamed by our superiors or our friends.

We should practice this meekness also toward ourselves. It is not praiseworthy to be provoked to anger against ourselves when we fall into some fault. It is a mistake. Such anger would keep us in a state of agitation, which renders us unfit for doing good.

Meekness is needed most of all whenever we are in duty bound to correct others. Corrections made with bitter zeal often do more harm than good, particularly when the person corrected is still excited. In that case we must refrain from making the correction for the moment, until the excitement of the moment dies down and tempers have cooled.

The same rule should be followed when we ourselves are in an angry mood. We should not make the correction just then; otherwise it will be made with angry words and bitter feelings, and the culprit, seeing himself treated in such a manner, will give little heed to the admonition given in anger. When we act in this way, we are thoughtful of the spiritual good of our neighbor.

As for our own spiritual good, let us show that we love Jesus Christ by accepting calmly and peacefully all inconsiderate treatment and insults.

PRAYER

Jesus, despised for love of me, from this day forward I will bear every affront for love of You. Give me the strength I need to keep this resolution.

My God and my all! I desire no other good except You who are the infinite good. You cared so much about my welfare; help me to care about nothing except Your good pleasure. Help me to avoid anything that might offend You and to do everything that will please You. Keep far from me anything that can turn me away from Your love.

Holy Virgin, my Mother Mary, I love you. I confide in you. Help me by your powerful intercession.

CHAPTER XII

LOVE WANTS WHAT GOD WANTS

A person who loves Jesus Christ truly, wants only what Jesus wants.

Love and truth are inseparable companions. Love knows that God is goodness itself; therefore it detests evil, which is opposed to the will of God, and it finds pleasure in nothing except what is pleasing to God.

The person who lives with the love of God in his heart bothers little about what others say of him; he gives all his attention to the task of pleasing God.

DOING THE WILL OF GOD

We have said repeatedly that holiness and perfection consist in overcoming self and in doing the will of God. Now let us discuss this truth in greater detail. If we wish to become saints this should be our never-changing program: never to follow our own will, but always to follow the will of God. That is the substance of all the divine counsels and commandments – to do and to suffer what God wills, as God wills. As we follow this program, we should all the while pray to God for liberty of spirit – the liberty of spirit which enables us to embrace everything that is pleasing to Jesus Christ no matter how unpleasant it may be to self-love or our regard for human respect.

The love of Jesus Christ gives to them who love Him a complete indifference: the bitter and the sweet are alike to them; they seek nothing to please themselves; they seek everything that is pleasing to God. They are equally content to occupy themselves in great affairs or matters of little importance; in pleasant things or in tasteless tasks. All they ask is to please God.

St. Augustine says: "Love God, and do what you please." Whoever really loves God seeks nothing but the good pleasure of God; he finds all his happiness in pleasing God.

St. Teresa writes: "How true it is, dear Lord, that all our troubles come from not keeping our eyes fixed on You! If we would only look to You, the true Way, how quickly we would have in our grasp that for which we are forever reaching! But we stumble and fall a thousand times as we try to go forward, and even stray off and get lost, because we fail to keep watching the true way." Say it a thousand times — and then once more — the only goal of all our thoughts, our actions, our desires, our prayers should be the good pleasure of God. This should be our road to holiness — to walk according to the will of God.

WITH OUR WHOLE HEART

God wants every one of us to love Him with our whole heart. "You shall love the Lord your God with your whole heart" (Matt. 22:37). With your whole heart! That person loves God with his whole heart who sincerely asks with the apostle: "Lord, what do you want me to do?" (Acts 9:6) Lord, tell me all that You want me to do, for I am determined to do it!

Let us understand well that when we want what God wants, we want what is best for ourselves; for God certainly wants nothing but what is for our good. St. Vincent de Paul said: "Conformity to the divine will is the treasure of Christians and the remedy for all ills because it embraces renunciation of self and union with God and the practice of every virtue." Right here, in fact, is all holiness: "Lord, what do You want me to do?"

St. Teresa said that the Lord never sends an affliction without rewarding it with some favor, if only we embrace the affliction with patience and in conformity with His divine will. Our conformity with the divine will, however, must be unconditional; we must not make any reservations or lay down conditions. It must be final, without recall. Here is the summit of holiness, and to attain it should be the purpose of all our activity, all our desires, all our prayers.

St. Teresa writes: "They deceive themselves who imagine that union with God consists in ecstasies, visions, the joys of sensible devotion. It consists in nothing else but the subjection of our will to the will of God."

COMPLAINTS

Many of us say: "Lord, I give You my entire will; I desire nothing but what You desire." But when God takes us at our word and lets trouble come, we cannot accept His will. Then we begin complaining. Bad luck always looks for us first! Life is nothing but gloom and unhappiness!

If we would persevere in our resolution to live according to the will of God in all adversities, we should certainly become holy. More than that, we should be the happiest persons in the world. Why not, therefore, keep trying day after day to keep our will united with God's will in everything that happens whether it is pleasing or distressing?

A saint said: "To take everything as it comes from the hand of God is an excellent means of preserving continual peace and tranquillity of heart. That is why the ancient fathers of the desert never gave evidence of being irritated or despondent; no matter what happened to them, they received each moment cheerfully from the hand of God."

WHO IS REALLY HAPPY?

Happiness is for those people who know how to live in total abandonment to the divine will. They are neither puffed up by success or crushed by failure, for they know that success and failure alike come from their loving Father's hand. God's will is the only rule of their life. They do only what God wills. They desire only what God desires. They do not undertake a multitude of tasks, since they are content to do perfectly whatever they believe God wants them to do. That is why they prefer the most trifling tasks of their state in life to great and glorious achievements; for they know that the latter might be prompted by self-love while the former are surely in accordance with the will of God.

We, too, shall be happy if we accept whatever God sends — accept it with perfect conformity to His divine will, not caring whether or not it is according to our natural likes and dislikes. One of the saints said: "When shall we finally learn to enjoy the sweetness of the divine will in everything that happens to us, considering nothing but the divine good pleasure, which certainly sends, with equal love and for our greater good, both adversity and prosperity? When shall we really throw ourselves into the arms of our most loving heavenly Father, abandoning unreservedly to Him the care of ourselves and of all that belongs to us, reserving for ourselves only the desire of pleasing God?"

St. Vincent de Paul developed the practice of self-control to such perfection that his friends used to say of him: "Vincent is always Vincent." What they meant was that the saint always remained calm and even-tempered no matter what happened. Whether success favored him or whether disappointment crushed him, his outward conduct and attitude were always tranquil. Because he had placed himself completely and confidently in the hands of God, and because he desired nothing except to give pleasure to God, he had nothing to fear.

SECRET OF HAPPINESS

St. Teresa writes: "When we place ourselves completely and finally in the hands of God, we are led into the charming land of peace and liberty of spirit, the homeland of those who seek to be perfect. In this land we are free to discover the secret of the greatest happiness that can be hoped for this side of heaven. They who dwell in this land fear nothing, seek nothing, desire nothing of the things of the world, but they possess all things."

But there are also many persons who prefer to remain in the small world of their own creation and they draw up their own plans for attaining holiness according to their personal ideas. The melancholy may seek holiness in a life of seclusion; the energetic will concentrate their efforts in works of zeal and charity; they who are inclined to severity may look for sanctity in penances and self-denial; the generous in almsgiving; others in reciting endless prayers; others in making pilgrimages to holy places. They conclude that holiness consists in making use of the means which they have chosen according to their personal inclinations. The external good works they perform ought really be the fruit of the love of Jesus Christ; but the love of Jesus Christ itself consists in entire conformity to His will and, consequently, in self-denial and the steadfast determination to please Him solely because He deserves it.

Others say they wish to serve God – but only in this particular place, with these certain friends, under these circumstances; and if things do not go according to their preference, they give up the good work they began or do it grudgingly. Such persons are not free with the true freedom of spirit; they are slaves of their own self-will, and therefore they gain little merit even for the good they do.

St. Francis de Sales writes: "Many indeed are they who say to the Lord, 'I give myself entirely to You without reserve.' But few are they who actually put this complete giving of self into practice. This abandonment consists in a certain indifference regarding everything that comes to us from God's providence, whether afflictions or consolations, whether contempt and insults or honor and praise."

EMOTION AND SENTIMENT

One of the saints used to say that all our prayers should have one object in view: to obtain from God the grace to follow His holy will in all things. There are some souls who suffer from a sort of spiritual gluttony. It seems that they can never satisfy their craving for spiritual sweetness. In their prayer they are looking only for the delights of consoling emotions and tender sentiments. But strong souls, souls who have a true desire to belong wholly to God, ask nothing from God but the light to know His will and the strength perfectly to do it.

PRAYER

Most amiable heart of my divine Savior, heart in love with men, heart loving us with such great tenderness, heart worthy to reign over our hearts and to possess them entirely, help me to understand more clearly how much you love me and all the souls in the world. My Jesus, please accept the offering and the sacrifice which I make to You this day as I once more sincerely offer to You my entire will. Tell me what You want me to do. Your holy grace will help me do it.

Mary, pray for me.

CHAPTER XIII

LOVE CAN TAKE IT!

Whoever loves Jesus Christ bears everything patiently for Jesus Christ, especially sickness, poverty and neglect.

We have previously discussed the practice of patience, but only in a summary way. Now we shall consider some individual cases in which patience is particularly needed.

PATIENCE IN ILLNESS

We shall speak first of all of sickness, pain and bodily infirmity, which, if we bear them with loving patience, will merit for us a rich reward in heaven.

St. Vincent de Paul said: "If we only knew the priceless treasures which are hidden in illness, we would accept it joyfully and consider it a great favor." Following his own advice, this saint, though tortured by endless maladies which often left him no rest either night or day, bore all his pain and discomfort with undisturbed peace. He seemed always to be in perfect health, for he never made the least complaint about his ills.

How unusual, but how edifying, is the sick man who always bears his infirmities with Christian calmness and serenity, as did St. Francis de Sales! When he was ill, he stated his condition and symptoms to the physician with all simplicity, punctually obeyed the doctor in taking the prescribed remedies, no matter how distasteful they might be, and then remained in peace, without lamenting or complaining to others. How different from those persons who complain without end about every little ailment and expect all their relatives and friends to crowd around them with expressions of sympathy!

St. Teresa advised her nuns: "Sisters, learn to suffer something for the Savior without publishing it to the world."

Many times we hear people say rather sorrowfully: "I am not unwilling to suffer this illness; but what makes me unhappy is that I can no longer go to church to perform my devotions, to receive Holy Communion frequently and to assist at the holy sacrifice of the Mass. I cannot even pray as I want to pray. My head aches so much and so constantly and I am so weak." Just a moment! Let me ask you one question. Why do you want to go to church? Why do you want to receive Holy Communion and assist at Mass? Is it to give pleasure to God? Well, for the present, while you are ill, it is not God's pleasure or will that you go to church or hear Mass, but that you patiently keep to your bed and bear the pain or discomfort of your sickness. If you cannot truly agree with what I say, then we must believe that what you are looking for is not what is pleasing to God, but what pleases you.

PRAYER IN SICKNESS

Sometimes a sick person will say that his illness is so painful that he cannot even pray. It is quite understandable that a feverish condition or great pain may make it impossible to make a meditation of some length or to say long prayers. But is it not possible to make short acts of resignation and conformity to the will of God? If these short prayers are frequently repeated they can unite to form an excellent meditation and will help the sick person to endure patiently the illness that afflicts him. This is what St. Vincent de Paul did when he was sick: he placed himself calmly in the presence of God, without trying to force his mind to consider anything in particular, making at intervals acts of love, confidence, thanksgiving and resignation to God's will.

You say you cannot pray when you are ill? What more beautiful prayer than an occasional glance at Christ on the cross? Offer Him the pain you feel, uniting your small suffering with the immense suffering He endured on the cross.

Whenever St. Teresa was afflicted with some infirmity, she was accustomed to say: "When I recall the great sufferings of Jesus, I do not see how I could ever begin to think of complaining about my little pains."

By bearing our infirmities patiently we can merit a great part, perhaps the greater part, of the reward which God will bestow upon us when we begin to live eternally in heaven.

Souls that fervently love Jesus Christ find suffering acceptable and even pleasing. That is why the holy martyrs went with such joy to meet their death by torture.

St. Procopius defied the tyrant who tormented him. "Torment me as much as you please; but let me tell you that for those who love Jesus Christ there is nothing more sweet than to suffer for Him."

Another martyr, St. Gordian, when threatened with death, replied: "Do you expect to frighten me by threatening me with death? My only regret is that I can die but once for Jesus Christ."

What was it that enabled the saints to speak in this manner? Were they insensible to pain? "No," says St. Bernard, "not insensibility, but love was the reason." They felt keenly the pain of the torments inflicted upon them, but because they loved God they considered it their greatest privilege to suffer everything, even death itself, for the love of God.

In time of sickness we should above all be ready to accept death — the death which God wills for us. We must die sometime, and our last sickness will end in death. Since we do not know which sickness will be our last, every time we become ill, we should prepare ourselves to accept willingly whatever death God has determined for us.

Someone may be inclined to say: "But I have committed so many sins and I have done no penance. I want to live, not for the sake of living, but in order to make some reparation to God before I die." But how do you know that by living longer you will do more penance and not commit more sins? At the present moment you can assuredly hope that God has pardoned you. What more appropriate penance could you possibly perform than to accept death with resignation, if God wills your death now?

St. Aloysius Gonzaga, dying at the age of 23, willingly met death in this spirit. "Today, as I hope, I am in the grace of God. Whether I shall remain so tomorrow, I do not know. Therefore I am glad to die now, if it pleases God to call me into the other world."

A good priest held the opinion that every Christian — even a moderately good Christian — should desire death in order to escape the danger in which everybody lives as long as he is on this earth of committing sin and losing the grace of God.

If we truly love God, we should long to go to see Him face to face and love Him with all our strength — something that nobody can do perfectly in this world. But until death opens the door for us, we cannot enter this home of eternal and perfect love. This thought made St. Augustine exclaim: "Lord, let me die; for unless I die, I cannot come to see You and love You face to face."

PATIENCE IN POVERTY

People who are poor in worldly possessions have an opportunity to practice great patience.

St. Augustine said: "He who has God has everything; he who does not have God has nothing."

Whoever possesses God and joins his will to the will of God finds every good thing in God. Think of St. Francis, who is called the poor man of Assisi. When he prayed, "My God and my all!" he considered himself richer than all the wealthy people in the world.

The saints were not only satisfied to be poor; they even tried to strip themselves of everything in order to guard themselves against attachment to the things of the world and to be united to God alone. If we do not have the generosity to give up all the goods of this world, let us at least be content with the possessions which God allows us to have. Let our concern be, not for earthly riches, but for the riches of heaven, which are immensely greater and which will last forever. Let us be convinced of the truth of that saying of St. Teresa: "The less we possess here, the more we shall enjoy there."

THE GOOD ROAD

Poverty is the straight and smooth road by which we travel easily to God. "Blessed," says the Lord, "are the poor in spirit, for theirs is the kingdom of heaven" (Matt. 5:3). In the other beatitudes, to the meek, to the pure of heart, He promises heaven in the next world, but to the poor in spirit He promises heaven – that is, a heavenly contentment – even in this life, "for theirs *is* the kingdom of heaven." This is true; for even here below the poor in spirit enjoy an anticipation of heaven. "Poor in spirit" means not only that they do not have the goods of this earth, but that they do not even desire them.

"Blessed poverty," says St. Lawrence Justinian, "which has nothing and fears nothing! Always merry and always abounding! It knows the secret of making every inconvenience profitable for heaven."

Jesus Christ said one day to Blessed Angela: "If poverty were not a great blessing, I would never have chosen it for myself, nor left it as an inheritance to My chosen ones." Indeed, it was the contemplation of Jesus in poverty that made the saints love to be poor.

"Not poverty, but the love of poverty," says St. Bernard, "is counted a virtue." For the poor in spirit God is always enough, and the things God gives are enough. The truly poor in spirit are glad even when they lack things which they need, for in that spirit lies the merit of poverty. Many are poor, but because they do not love their poverty, they merit nothing.

DEATH OF LOVED ONES

The loss of relatives and friends by death must be endured with patience. There are some persons who do not know how to reconcile themselves to the death of a relative or friend. Lacking patience in such a trial, they spend days and days in tears and despondency until their conduct becomes quite unreasonable and inexcusable. I should like to ask such persons, who carry their mourning and grief to such excess, "Is your unrestrained mourning and weeping pleasing to God? Certainly not to God; for God wants us to be resigned to His will. Do you by your excessive grief offer any consolation or assistance to the soul that has departed into eternity? No! If that soul is saved and already in heaven, it wants you to join it in thanking God. If it is in purgatory, it desires that you assist it by your prayers and that you conform yourself to God's will and make use of the time you still have to sanctify yourself, so that you may come one day to join it in heaven."

When the sorrow at the death of a loved one comes to us, we should imitate Job. When he received word of the death of his children, he said with full resignation to God's will: "The Lord has given, and the Lord has taken away. It was God who gave me those children, and it is God who takes them. As it has pleased the Lord, so is it done. Blessed be the name of the Lord!"

PATIENCE IN NEGLECT

God wants us to practice patience when we are ignored, slighted or insulted.

One day an angel appeared to Blessed Henry Suso and said to him: "Henry, until now you have been mortifying yourself; from now on others will mortify you." On the following day, while standing at a window, he saw a dog holding a rag in its teeth and tearing it to shreds. Then he heard a voice: "It is in this way that you will be cut and torn by the tongues of men." Blessed Henry then went down to the place where the scattered shreds of the rag had been left by the dog; he gathered up the pieces carefully and kept them to remind himself of the need of courage in the coming days of trial.

For 30 years St. Philip Neri had to put up with much ill-treatment while he lived in the house dedicated to St. Jerome in the city of Rome; but it was just for that reason that he refused to leave this house and accept the invitation of his brethren of the Oratory to come and live with them in the place called Chiesa Nuova, which he himself had founded. When he finally yielded, it was only out of obedience to an express command of the pope.

These examples show us how the saints reached the point at which they desired and welcomed unkind treatment.

COURAGE NEEDED

St. Teresa gave us this forceful saying: "Whoever aspires to holiness must be careful never to say: 'They have no reason to treat me in this way.' If you are not willing to be badly dealt with except when there is a reason, then holiness is not for you."

Insults, poverty, suffering and trials of all kinds serve only to estrange further from God the soul that does not love Him; but coming to a soul that truly loves God, they serve to increase its love and to unite it more closely to Him. "Many waters cannot quench charity" (Cant. 8:7). Afflictions, be they ever so great and so many, do not extinguish, but rather brighten the flames of love in a heart that loves God and God alone.

In order to practice patience in all our tribulations we must be convinced that they come either directly from the hand of God, or indirectly through the instrumentality of men. When afflictions come upon us, we should thank the Lord for them, and we should accept willingly and gladly whatever He sends — favors or crosses — because He sends all for our good. "To them that love God all things work together unto good" (Rom. 8:28).

To suffer calls for courage. Where shall we find the courage to bear with patience every pain, every insult, every adversity? Not so much in involved processes of reasoning and in looking for satisfying explanations, but rather in prayer. The divine help that will be given in answer to our prayer will supply the strength we lack.

PRAYER

Dear Lord, I am now convinced that without patient suffering I cannot merit a reward in heaven. It is You who must give me patience in suffering. I make the resolution to accept with patience all the trials and sufferings that will come into my life. I know that so often, in spite of my resolutions, I have become despondent when I was asked to carry a cross; but if I do not learn to suffer for love of You, I shall suffer without merit. My Jesus, by the merits of the patience with which You suffered so many pains for love of me, give me the grace to bear my crosses for love of You.

Mary, my Queen, obtain for me true and loving resignation in everything I still have to suffer in life and at death.

CHAPTER XIV

LOVE BELIEVES ALL THINGS

Whoever loves Jesus Christ believes all His words.

A lover puts faith in everything said by the beloved. The greater our love is for Jesus Christ, the stronger and more alive will be our faith in Him.

The good thief, seeing our Redeemer dying on the cross and suffering with so much patience, even though He had done no wrong, began to love Him; and because he allowed this beginning of love to grow within him he was assisted by the grace of God to repent of his sins, to believe that Christ was truly the Son of God and to beg Him to remember him when He came into His kingdom.

Love is built on faith, but faith is brought to perfection by love. The more perfectly one loves God, the more perfectly he believes.

Sinners believe only too well in the truths of faith, but they will not live according to the divine commandments. They believe only with the intellect and not with the will. Their faith is weak. If they had a strong living faith whereby they really believed that divine grace is a good greater than every other good, and that sin, which deprives us of divine grace, is an evil greater than every other evil, they would surely change their life. If some persons choose the goods and pleasures of the world in preference to the friendship of God, they do so because they have no faith, or because their faith has grown quite feeble.

THE WILL TO BELIEVE

On the contrary, he who believes not only with his intellect, but also with his will, so that he not only believes, but has the will to believe in God, the revealer of truth, because of the love he has for God, and rejoices in so believing, such a person has a perfect faith and as a result tries to make his life conform to the truths that he believes.

The weak faith of persons who live sinful lives is not due to the obscurity of the teachings of faith. God has, indeed, willed that for us the truths of faith should be obscured and hidden so that we might acquire merit by believing them; but at the same time the evidence offered us that the teachings of faith are true is so convincing that to refuse to believe them is not merely a lack of good sense; it is madness.

In many cases a weak faith is the result of an evil life. They who reject the divine friendship rather than deprive themselves of the forbidden satisfaction of their desires, would be only too happy if there were no law to hold them back and no chastisement to punish their sins. Therefore they try to blind themselves to the eternal truths of death, judgment, hell and the divine justice. Because the eternal truths are too terrifying and embitter his sinful gratifications, the sinner sets his mind to work to discover some believable argument whereby he can convince himself, or hoodwink himself into believing that there is no God, no soul, no hell — so that he can live and die like the animals who have no moral laws or rational minds to guide them.

EXCUSES

To find comforting excuses for sinful living, some will say that there is no God. Others deny divine providence — saying that after creating man, God no longer concerns himself about what we do, whether we love Him, or whether we offend Him, or whether we are damned.

Who can understand the ingratitude and malice of sinners? God, in His goodness, has created them to be eternally happy in heaven; He has poured out upon them in abundance so many talents, favors and graces to help them earn eternal salvation; He has redeemed them at the price of so much pain and such great love; but they deliberately blind themselves to all these favors so that they may follow their evil inclinations and live in sin. Let them try as they will, these ungrateful children of a loving Father can never free themselves from the remorse of a bad conscience or from the fear of divine retribution. If sinners would only abandon their evil ways and surrender themselves to the love of Jesus Christ, they would no longer try to deny or escape the teachings of faith, but would firmly believe all the truths which God has revealed.

Whoever loves Jesus Christ keeps always before his mind the eternal truths and lives according to them. Whoever loves Jesus Christ understands well the saying of the Wise Man: "Vanity of vanities, and all is vanity." The glory offered by the world allures us, but it passes quickly away and brings only deceit and disappointment. The treasure of happiness is to be found only in loving God and doing His will. We are what we are before God. It profits nothing to gain the entire world and lose one's soul. All the goods of the earth cannot satisfy the human heart; God alone, and His friendship, can bring contentment to the heart of man. Great is our success if we lose all to gain All.

Yes, love believes all things.

PART-TIME FAITH

There are some Christians who believe, but their faith is a sort of part-time faith; their faith blows hot and cold; their faith believes only what it chooses to believe. They believe the sacred mysteries; they believe the truths revealed in the Gospels — the Trinity, the redemption, the sacraments; but they do not believe all. Jesus Christ said: "Blessed are the poor in spirit; blessed are the sorrowful; blessed are they who endure persecution." This is the teaching of Christ's Gospel. But how can anyone pretend to believe in that Gospel when he contradicts these statements of Christ? It is a contradiction of the Gospel to say in word or by action: "Blessed is he that has money. Blessed is he who has nothing to suffer. Blessed is he who can enjoy himself. Unhappy is he who is persecuted or treated badly."

They who speak in this manner, either do not believe in the Gospels at all or they believe them only in part. Whoever believes completely in the Gospels and believes sincerely in the words of Jesus Christ, will always see God's blessing hand in sickness, misfortune, neglect, sorrow and a lack of worldly possessions. Such faith, however, must always find its strength and its life in a true love for Jesus Christ.

PRAYER

Beloved Redeemer, life of my soul, I believe that You alone are worthy of all my love. I believe that You are the greatest lover of my soul, for impelled by love alone, You have permitted yourself to be drowned in sufferings and You have given Your life for love of me. I believe that in this life there is no better thing that I can do than to love You and to do Your will. All this I believe firmly. I am willing to give up everything else rather than give up my love for You. By the merits of Your sufferings help me and make my love for You the kind of love You want it to be.

Refuge of sinners, Mary, Mother of God, pray for me.

CHAPTER XV

LOVE HOPES FOR ALL THINGS

Whoever loves Jesus Christ hopes for all things from Him.

Hope increases love, and love increases hope. There can be no doubt that hope in the divine goodness increases love for Jesus Christ. St. Thomas tells us that when we begin to hope for something from somebody, in that very moment we begin to love him. That is why the Lord does not want us to put our hope in creatures. "Put not your trust in princes" (Ps. 145:3).

· St. Vincent de Paul said: "We should guard against too much reliance on men, for the Lord, when He sees us thus depending on them, withdraws from us." On the contrary, the more we trust Him, the more we grow in His love.

The man whose heart is great with confidence in God, runs on the road to holiness. Not only does he run, he flies, for having put all his hope in the Lord, he ceases to be weak, as he was formerly; he becomes strong with God's own strength, which is communicated to all who trust in God. "They that hope in the Lord shall renew their strength; they shall take wings as eagles; they shall run and not be weary; they shall walk and not faint" (Is. 40:31).

Just as hope supports us and makes us grow in the love of God, so does love increase our hope, for love makes us adopted children of God. In the natural order we are the creatures of God's hands; but in the supernatural order, through the merits of Jesus Christ, we have been made sons of God and partakers of the divine nature, as St. Peter writes: "That by these you may be made partakers of the divine nature" (2 Peter 1:4). If love makes us sons of God, it consequently makes us also heirs of heaven, according to the words of St. Paul: "And if sons, heirs also" (Rom. 8:17). Now sons have a right to live in their father's house; heirs have a right to inherit. Therefore our love for God strengthens our hope of heaven. That is why loving souls ceaselessly call out to God: "Thy kingdom come! Thy kingdom come!"

ALWAYS CHEERFUL

God loves those who love Him. He showers graces on those that seek Him with love. "The Lord is good to the soul that seeks Him" (Jer. 31:25). From this it follows that whoever has more love for God, has more hope in His goodness; and of such confidence is born that undisturbed tranquillity which enables the saints to remain always cheerful and unruffled in the midst of affliction; for loving Jesus Christ and knowing how liberal He is toward those who love Him, in Him alone they put their trust and find their repose.

The primary object of Christian hope is God — God enjoyed in the kingdom of the blessed. But we must never imagine that the hope of enjoying God in heaven can interfere with love; for the hope of heaven is inseparably connected with love, which is made perfect in heaven and finds its completeness there.

St. Thomas writes that the true foundation of friendship is the mutual interchange of benefits. Since friendship is nothing else than a mutual love between friends, it is necessary that they mutually do good to each other as the situation dictates or indicates. Therefore St. Thomas says: "Where there is no interchange of benefits, there is no friendship." For this reason Jesus Christ said to His disciples: "I have called you friends, because all things whatsoever I have heard from My Father I have made known to you" (John 15:15). Since He had made His disciples His friends, He had made known to them His secrets.

GREATER LOVE — STRONGER HOPE

"Love hopes all things." Christian hope, as defined by St. Thomas, is a certain expectation of eternal happiness. This certainty is born of the infallible promise of God to give eternal life to His faithful servants. Now love, since it takes away sin, takes away at the same time the impediment to the attaining of happiness. Therefore, the greater our love, the greater and stronger is our hope.

A soul that dearly loves Jesus Christ, cannot, so long as it is on this earth, refrain from desiring to go quickly to heaven to unite itself with its beloved Lord. Therefore the desire to go to see God in heaven, not so much for the joy we shall there experience in loving God, as for the joy we shall give to God in loving Him, is pure and perfect love. Neither does the joy, which the blessed feel in loving God, take away from the purity of their love; such joy is inseparable from love. But the blessed souls delight principally much more in the love they bear to God than in the joy they feel in loving Him.

But, you may object, to desire the reward is love of concupiscence, and not of friendship. You must distinguish between the temporal rewards promised by men and the reward of heaven promised by God to those that love Him. The rewards which men give, are distinct from their persons, because men, when they reward their fellows, give not themselves but only their goods. On the contrary, the principal reward which God gives to the blessed is himself. Therefore desiring heaven is the same thing as desiring God, who is our final end.

"You shall love the Lord, your God, with your whole heart, and with your whole soul, and with all your strength" (Luke 10:27). St. Thomas says that men cannot perfectly fulfill this commandment so long as they are on earth. Only Jesus Christ, who was Man and God, and most holy Mary, who was full of grace and free from original sin, perfectly fulfilled this comandment. But we cannot love God without some imperfection. Only in heaven, when we see Him face to face, shall we be able to love Him – indeed, we shall find ourselves compelled to love Him – with all our strength.

THE GREAT PURPOSE

This is the goal toward which we must direct all our desires, all our longings, all our thoughts, all our hopes: to go and enjoy God in heaven in order to love Him with all our strength and to rejoice in His joy.

The souls of the blessed in heaven rejoice in their own happiness. That is quite true. But their principal rejoicing, which absorbs all their other joys, is that of knowing the infinite happiness enjoyed by their beloved Lord, for they love Him immensely more than they love themselves.

The moment a soul enters heaven and sees revealed in the light of glory the infinite beauty of God, it feels completely overpowered and consumed by love. At that moment it is happily lost and submerged in the infinite ocean of the divine goodness; then it forgets itself and, filled with the love of God, it thinks of nothing but of loving its God. The blessed think of nothing but of loving and pleasing the beloved; they desire to possess Him entirely, and they do already possess Him without fear of ever losing Him again; they desire to give themselves to Him at every moment, all for love. And they realize this desire, for at every moment they do give themselves to Him without reserve, and God embraces them with love, and in that embrace He holds them, and will hold them for all eternity.

In this manner the soul is completely united to God in heaven and loves Him with all its strength. The soul's love is most perfect and complete, and though it is necessarily limited, since a creature is not capable of infinite love, it nevertheless causes the soul to be perfectly happy and contented, so that it desires nothing more.

On the other hand, almighty God communicates himself and unites himself wholly to the soul, filling it with himself according to the measure of the soul's merits; and God unites himself to the soul, now no longer merely by His gifts, inspirations and attractions, as He does in this life, but by His own very essence.

HAPPINESS IN GOD

As fire penetrates iron and seems to transform the iron into itself, so God penetrates the soul and fills it with himself. The soul, while it does not lose its own existence, nevertheless becomes so saturated and absorbed in that immense ocean of the divine substance that it becomes, as it were, annihilated and deprived of existence. That is the state of happiness which the apostle begged for his followers. "That you may be filled unto all the fullness of God" (Eph. 3:19).

This is the final goal which God in His goodness has willed we should reach in the world to come. The soul can never enjoy perfect repose on earth, because it is only in heaven that it can obtain perfect union with God. It is true that the soul which loves Jesus Christ, finds peace in conforming its will to the divine will; but it can never, in this life, find complete repose, for that can be obtained only by reaching its final destiny, which is to see God face to face and to be consumed by divine love. So long as the soul has not reached that final goal, it is restless and mourning and weeping.

Yes, my God, I am resigned to live in this valley of tears, because such is Your will; but I cannot help feeling inexpressible bitterness in seeing myself still far from You and not yet perfectly united to You, my destiny, my all, my complete repose.

The saints, though they were aflame with love of God here on earth, nevertheless carefully sighed for heaven. David exclaimed: "Woe is me that my sojourning is prolonged" (Ps. 119:5). "I shall be satisfied when Thy glory shall appear" (Ps. 16:15).

PRAYER

O God, my Creator and my Redeemer, You have created me for heaven.

O my Jesus, would that I had never offended You, that I had always loved You!

My consolation is that I still have time to love You.

I love You, O soul of my soul, I love You with all my heart. I love You more than myself.

I know that You wish me to be saved so that I may love You for all eternity in Your kingdom of love. I thank You, and I beg You to help me during the remainder of my life during which I wish to love You exceedingly in order to love You exceedingly in eternity.

My Jesus, when will that day arrive when I shall know that I am secure against the danger of losing You and when, consumed by love, I shall see revealed Your infinite beauty and shall feel myself constrained to love You?

O Queen of Heaven, Mary, your intercession is so powerful with God. I place my hope in you.

CHAPTER XVI

LOVE IS NOT AFRAID

Whoever loves Jesus Christ with an ardent love does not cease loving Him no matter how severely he is tempted or how completely he feels abandoned.

The pains felt most keenly in this world by those who love God are not poverty, illness, disgrace or persecution, but temptations and desolation of spirit.

When a soul enjoys the loving presence of God, all pains, outrages and mean treatment lead the soul not into a state of sadness but consolation; for they afford the soul an opportunity of giving God a pledge of its love. We can say that such afflictions and trials add fuel to the flames of love. But when these souls feel themselves impelled by temptation to forfeit divine grace, or when in their desolation they fear that they have already surrendered the friendship of God, they suffer bitterly.

Such souls love Jesus with all their heart and they dread nothing more than separation from the God they love. Their love, however, gives them strength to suffer with patience and to continue blindly to walk on the road to perfection during these trials which God permits them to suffer in order to prove their love.

TEMPTATIONS

They who love Jesus Christ sincerely can suffer no greater pain than that which is caused by temptation to sin. All other trials, if accepted with resignation, help to unite them more intimately with God. But temptations to sin urge them to separate themselves completely from Jesus Christ. That is why temptations are more bitter than any other torment.

Note well, however, that no temptation to sin ever comes from God, but always from the devil or from our own evil inclinations, "for God is not a tempter of evil, and He tempts no man" (James 1:13). Nevertheless the Lord does at times permit His dearest friends to be grievously tempted.

One reason why God permits those who love Him to be tempted is that they may better learn their own weakness and the need they have of divine help to keep from falling into sin. When a soul realizes that it is being favored by God with divine consolations, it feels capable of overcoming every assault of the enemy and of accomplishing any undertaking for the glory of God; but when it is fiercely tempted and finds itself on the brink of the precipice and in imminent danger of falling, then it understands better its misery and its helplessness to resist, if God does not come to its aid.

LONGING OF THE SOUL

Again, God permits temptations so that we may live more detached from the world and that we may desire more ardently to go to see Him in heaven. Faithful souls, seeing themselves attacked day and night by so many enemies, grow weary of life and exclaim: "Woe is me that my sojourning is prolonged" (Ps. 119:5). They long for the hour in which they can say: "The snare is broken, and we are delivered" (Ps. 123:7). The soul longs to fly to God, but so long as it lives on this earth it is entangled in a snare that holds it here where it is constantly assailed by temptations. This snare will be broken only by death. That is why loving souls long for death, because death will free them from the danger of losing God.

Then, too, God permits us to be tempted to make us more rich in merits. The angel told Tobias:

"Because you were acceptable to God, it was necessary that temptation should prove you" (Tob. 12:13). Nobody should think that, just because he is tempted, he has fallen into disgrace with God; on the contrary, he should look upon it as an indication that he is more loved by God.

It is a trick of the devil to make certain worrisome persons imagine that temptations are sins and that they soil the soul. It is not the evil imagination, but the evil consent, that makes us lose God. The suggestions of the devil may be ever so strong, the impure images that cross the mind may be ever so vivid, but so long as we do not deliberately want them, they have no power to soil the soul; on the contrary, if we calmly repel them, they make us purer, stronger, dearer to God.

Neither should we worry if the tempting evil thoughts will not leave us, even though we try to turn them away. If these thoughts continue to torment us, it is sufficient that we detest them and try to get rid of them.

"God is faithful, who will not suffer you to be tempted above that which you are able, but will make also with the temptation issue, that you may be able to bear it" (1 Cor. 10:13).

REWARD AND MERIT

Whenever we resist a temptation we lose nothing; rather we gain a reward. That is why the Lord often permits the souls that are dearer to Him to be more tormented by temptations, for by overcoming the temptations they earn more merit in this world and glory in heaven.

Stagnant water that is never stirred up soon becomes putrid. So, too, the soul, when it grows lazy because it has encountered no temptations, is in danger of falling into vain complacency over its supposed holiness, imagining that it has already arrived at perfection. Thinking that it has little to fear from its own weakness, it seldom recommends itself to God and makes little effort to make sure of its eternal salvation.

When, however, a soul is buffeted by temptation and sees itself in danger of being overcome by sin, it flies for refuge to God and to the Mother of God; it protests again and again that it is resolved to die rather than commit sin; it humbles itself and abandons itself to the arms of divine mercy. In this manner it acquires new strength and binds itself more closely to God, as experience shows.

Now this does not mean that we should wish for temptations; on the contrary, we should constantly pray to God to deliver us from temptations, and above all from those temptations which God foresees might conquer us.

TRUST IN GOD

When God permits temptations to attack us, then, without giving way to nervous panic on account of the ugliness and strength of the temptation, or giving way to discouragement, we should put our trust in Jesus Christ and seek His help. Assuredly He will not fail to give us the help and strength we need to resist the temptation. St. Augustine says: "Put your trust in God and fear nothing. If God sends you into the combat, He certainly will not leave you to be defeated."

Now let us see what means we should use to overcome temptation.

Spiritual guides enumerate many means to be used against temptation. The most necessary means and the most efficacious means, and the only means of which I intend to speak is to have prompt recourse to

God with humility and confidence, saying: "Come to my aid, O God! O Lord, help me quickly!" With this prayer alone we can overcome the attacks of all the devils in hell, because God is infinitely stronger than all the devils. God knows well that we do not have the strength to repel the temptations of the infernal powers. Whenever we are attacked and are in danger of being overcome, God is obliged to give us enough strength to resist, provided we ask Him for help.

How can we ever fear that Jesus Christ will fail us after all the promises He has made us in holy Scripture? "Come to me, all you that labor and are heavily burdened, and I will refresh you" (Matt. 11:28). Come to Me, you that have grown weary in fighting temptations, and I will restore your strength. "Call upon me in the day of trouble; I will deliver you, and you shall honor me" (Ps. 49:15). When you are assailed by the enemy, call out to Me, and I will save you from the danger. Then will you glorify Me.

Who, asks the prophet, has ever called upon God for help and found that God despised his petition and sent no help?

David believed that, when he used this great means of prayer, he would never be overcome by his enemies. "Praising, I shall call upon the Lord, and I shall be saved from my enemies" (Ps. 17:4). David knew well that God is near to all who pray to Him. "The Lord is nigh to all them that call upon him" (Ps. 144:18). St. Paul adds that the Lord is not miserly but lavish with His graces toward all that ask for them. "Rich unto all that call upon him" (Rom. 10:12).

EXPERIENCE OF PRAYER

If all men would only call upon God when they are tempted to sin, surely nobody would ever offend

Him. Some fall miserably because, when they are tempted by their evil inclinations, rather than deny themselves these brief satisfactions, they prefer to lose God, the supreme good. Experience proves over and over that whoever prays in temptation conquers, and whoever does not pray falls, especially in temptations against chastity.

Solomon said: "As I knew that I could not otherwise be continent except God gave it, I went to the Lord and besought him" (Wis. 8:21). In temptations to impurity — and the same holds for temptations against faith — it is not wise strategy to grapple directly with the temptation; one should at the very beginning of the temptation take care to repel it indirectly by making an act of the love of God or an act of contrition; or one should distract the mind by turning one's attention to some indifferent action.

The very moment we notice a thought that has an ugly look, we should throw it out and slam the door in its face without dallying to ask who it is and what it wants — but promptly, but immediately — just as we would brush a spark of fire from our clothing.

We should ask the Lord to come to our aid, invoking the holy names of Jesus and Mary, which have a special power and efficacy to dispel such temptations. Do not stop to consider the temptation. Do not argue with it.

If the temptation still continues to trouble us, we must continue to invoke Jesus and Mary. It helps much when temptation continues trying to draw us into sin, to renew our promise to God to be faithful to Him. At the same time we should continue to beg God to give us strength to keep this promise.

A GOOD RULE

It is good to note here that, according to the common teaching of the theologians, even the theologians who are more strict, that those who for some time have lived a spiritual life and are deeply imbued with the fear of God, when in doubt, and not certain, of having given consent to a serious sin, should hold for certain that they have not lost divine grace.

Here is the reason for this statement: it is morally impossible for anyone who, for a long time, has been firm in his good resolutions, suddenly to change his dispositions and consent to serious sin without knowing it clearly. St. Teresa said: "Nobody will be lost without knowing it."

St. Jane de Chantal relates that, having been disturbed for years by terrifying tempests of temptation and never being certain that she had consented to them, she had never confessed them, but had followed the rule given to her by her director. These are her words: "I was never fully certain that I had consented." From this it is clear that she was troubled for fear she might have consented, but nevertheless she found peace in obeying her director who had commanded her not to confess these doubtful sins.

Now I repeat: among all the remedies against temptation, the most efficacious and the most necessary, the remedy of remedies, is to pray to God for help – to pray, and to continue to pray, as long as the temptation continues. Often the Lord has decreed to give us the victory in answer not to the first prayer, but to the second, to the third, to the fourth. We must be convinced that on prayer depends our amendment of life, on prayer depends our victory over temptations, on prayer depends our attaining divine love, on prayer we must rely for reaching holiness, receiving the grace of perseverance and possessing eternal salvation.

Without the help of God we do not have the strength to resist the attacks of the devil and for this reason the apostle exhorts us to put on the armor of God.

"Put on the armor of God that you may be able to stand against the deceits of the devil. For our wrestling is not against flesh and blood, but against principalities and powers, against the rulers of the world of this darkness" (Eph. 6:11-12).

What is this armor? This armor is continual and fervent prayer to God to aid us and not to let us suffer defeat.

Furthermore, I know that all the Scriptures never cease urging us to pray. "Call upon me, and I will deliver you" (Ps. 49:15). "Cry to me, and I will hear you" (Jer. 33:3). "We ought always to pray and not to faint" (Luke 18:1). "Ask and you shall receive" (Matt. 7:7). "Watch and pray" (Matt. 26:41). "Pray without ceasing" (1 Thess. 5:17).

I know of course that in the spiritual life we get great help from sermons, meditations, from the sacrifice of the Mass, Communions and mortifications; but when temptation comes, if we do not recommend ourselves to God, we shall fall, in spite of all the sermons, in spite of all the meditations, in spite of all the Masses and Communions, in spite of all our penances and good resolutions.

Therefore, if we want to be saved, let us always recommend ourselves to our Redeemer, Jesus Christ, and especially in the moment of temptation. Let us beg Him, not only to give us the grace of holy perseverance, but also the grace always to pray for perseverance.

Furthermore, let us always recommend ourselves to the Mother of God, who is, says St. Bernard, the dispenser of all graces. "Let us seek grace, and let us seek it through Mary." At the same time the saint assures us that it is God's will that we should not receive a single grace that does not pass through the hands of Mary.

TRIALS AND CONSOLATIONS

St. Francis de Sales tells us that we deceive ourselves when we try to measure our piety by the spiritual consolations we experience. Solid piety consists in a resolute will to do everything that God wants. God has a way of drawing to himself the souls He loves most by permitting them to experience dryness and desolation.

In order to reach true union with God the soul must give up its tendency to pamper its inordinate inclinations. When the Lord desires to draw a soul to His perfect love, He seeks to detach it from all affection for created things. He continues, little by little, to detach the soul from everything created, so that it finally will place all its affections in Him.

Then to draw the soul to the love of spiritual goods, He allows the soul, in the beginning, to taste great spiritual sweetness. The soul seeks to detach itself from the pleasures of sense; it may even yearn to afflict itself with penances and fasts.

That is why persons who begin sincerely and earnestly to strive for a higher spiritual life should not be surprised or disappointed if their confessor or director is sparing in granting permission to perform bodily penances. It is right that he should urge them to perform interior mortifications by accepting with patience the little and the many unpleasant things that happen in the course of every day; by being faithful in the performance of the smallest duties; by restraining their curiosity and not trying to see and hear everything, and similar practices. When they have acquired the habit of performing these interior mortifications or penances, then they will be ready and prepared to perform greater and exterior acts of penance.

DO NOT DESIRE CONSOLATIONS

But to return to our subject: when a soul begins to give itself to God and to taste the sweetness of sensible consolation with which the Lord tries to draw it away from worldly pleasures, it gradually detaches itself from creatures and begins to unite itself with God. But there is a defect in its attachment to God, for it is drawn more by the sensible satisfaction found in these spiritual consolations than by a firm will to please God, and it tricks itself into believing that the more sweetness it finds in its devotions, the more it loves God. And so, when it is called away from some practice of devotion in which it finds its spiritual delights, in order to perform some work or duty, it becomes troubled and sad. This is a universal weakness of our poor human nature: to seek in everything our own satisfaction.

Or it may happen, too, that when the soul no longer finds the usual spiritual delights in these devotional acts, it quits them, or at least shortens them; and so, day by day shortening them more and more, it ends by giving them up entirely.

This is the tragic experience of many souls called by God to His love. They begin to walk on the road to holiness and really make some progress so long as they taste spiritual sweetness; but when the sweetness vanishes, they give up all their efforts to give themselves truly to God and then return to their former ordinary way of life. We must be firmly convinced that love of God and holiness do not consist in feeling tender emotions and rapturous consolations, but in suppressing self-love and doing the will of God. St. Francis de Sales says that God deserves equal love when He consoles us and when He tries us.

COLDNESS, DARKNESS, WORRY

There is no great virtue in giving up the pleasures of sense and bearing contradictions while enjoying great consolations. While tasting such sweetness the soul suffers everything with patience; but often that patience is furnished more by the sweet flavor of these spiritual delights than by the strength of the love of God in the soul. That is why the good Lord, in order to strengthen such a soul in virtue, removes the feeling of His presence from it and deprives it of those sentiments of spiritual joy, in order to free it from all attachment to self-love and self-satisfaction which had been fed by such feelings.

Where formerly the soul found satisfaction in making acts of self-offering, of confidence, of love, now, since the fountain is dry, it can make these acts only with coldness and difficulty, and it feels disgust in the most pious practices – in prayer, in spiritual reading, in offering the Mass, in Communion. What is even worse, it experiences nothing but darkness and worry, and it seems that all contact with God is lost. The soul prays and prays, and then it is plunged into sad affliction, for seemingly God does not even hear its prayer.

WHAT WE SHOULD DO ON OUR PART

When the Lord in His mercy consoles us with His loving visits and makes us feel the activity of His grace within us, it is not right to reject these divine consolations. We should receive them with gratitude; but at the same time we should take good care not to halt our onward march in order to linger over the enjoyment of these spiritual caresses. That would be what St. John of the Cross calls spiritual gluttony. It is not pleasing to God. We ought rather, on such occasions, dismiss from our mind any complacency in this sweetness which is pleasing to our senses or emotions, and above all we must be on our guard not to imagine that God is treating us with this delicate attention because we are better than others. Such vain thoughts would force the Lord to withdraw from us entirely and leave us plodding along in our misery.

We should, indeed, offer fervent thanks to God for such sweetness if it is given to us, because these spiritual consolations are great gifts of God, unspeakably more to be treasured than all earthly riches and honors; but we should not stop to dally with the resultant sense pleasure or emotion; rather we should humble ourselves and recall our past sins.

We should persuade ourselves that these are simply gifts from the goodness of God, and that perhaps the Lord has seen fit to encourage us by these consolations so that later on we might be able to bear with patience some heavy cross He intends to send us. In moments of peace and consolation and even spiritual sweetness, we ought to make use of the opportunity to offer ourselves to suffer every pain that may come to us, whether pain of soul or of body, every infirmity, every trial, every anguish of spirit, saying:

"My Lord, here I am. Do with me and with all that belongs to me whatever You please. Give me the grace to love You and perfectly to do Your will, and I will ask for nothing else."

TIME OF TESTING

When a soul is morally certain that it is in the grace of God, even though it may be deprived of all natural and supernatural pleasures, it is happy in its condition, for it knows that it loves God and is loved by God. But God, who wishes to see that soul still more purified and detached from all sensible satisfaction in order to be completely united to Him by pure love, permits the soul to experience a feeling of desolation.

The pain of this desolation may be more bitter than all other exterior or interior pains which a soul can suffer. God deprives the soul of all assurance that it is in the state of grace. He leaves it in heavy darkness where it can no longer find its God. Sometimes God permits the soul to be attacked by fierce temptations of the flesh and by strong inclinations toward base gratifications, or by thoughts of unbelief or of despair, or even by thoughts of hatred against God, since it feels that God has cast it off and no longer listens to its prayers.

Because the suggestions of the devil are quite vehement at such a time, and because the inclinations to evil are strongly aroused, the soul, even though it resists with the will, is in such darkness that it cannot discern whether it has resisted or consented. Then the soul is troubled by an increasing fear that it has lost God, and that, on account of its infidelity in this struggle, God has, with good reason, completely abandoned it. This pain was endured by St. Teresa; and the saint admitted that while she was in this condition, solitude was no longer a solace and that when she tried to pray, she experienced great torments of soul.

When this happens to a soul that loves God, it should by no means lose heart. Those sensual inclinations, those temptations against faith, those thoughts of despair and feelings of hatred of God — all these are only fears; they are torments of soul; they are efforts of the enemy to overcome our resistance. But they are not acts of the will, and therefore they are not sins. The soul that truly loves Jesus Christ really does resist; it refuses consent to these evil suggestions; but, because it is in darkness, the soul cannot see and judge clearly, and it remains confused. Because it seems to be deprived of grace, it feels abandoned.

Even though souls thus tried by God may be saturated with fear, such fear is groundless. Ask these persons, even when they feel hopelessly abandoned, whether they would, with open eyes, deliberately commit even one venial sin, and they will resolutely answer that they are ready to suffer any trial rather than deliberately to offer any offense to God.

Note well that it is one thing to perform a good act of the will, such as to reject a temptation, to trust in God, to love and desire what God desires, and that it is quite another thing to know clearly that we have performed such an act. To be certain that we have performed a good act serves to give us satisfaction; but our genuine profit is in really performing the good act.

OUR WILL AND THE WILL OF GOD

To sum up: let us never imagine, when we feel increased spiritual consolation, that we are more loved by God, because holiness consists, not in feeling spiritual sweetness but in uniting our will with the will of God.

St. Teresa writes: "The Lord tests those who love Him with dryness and temptations. Though the dryness lasts a lifetime, never give up prayer. The day will come when you will be generously repaid."

Let them take courage then, those souls dear to God, souls who find themselves alone in desolation, deprived of all consolation, but who at the same time are determined to belong to God alone. Their desolation is a sign that God loves them tenderly and that He is keeping in readiness a place for them in heaven where consolations are complete and everlasting. Let such souls be assured and comforted by the knowledge that the more they are afflicted in this world, the more will they be consoled in their Father's home in heaven. "According to the multitude of my sorrows in my heart, your comforts have given joy to my soul" (Ps. 93:19).

For the consolation of persons whom God permits to be purified by the trials of desolation I now relate the experience of St. Jane de Chantal. For 41 years St. Jane was tormented by terrible spiritual sufferings; by temptations; by fears of having lost the friendship of God and of having been abandoned by Him. So continuous and so intense was her anguish that she was led to say that the only thing that gave her a moment's peace was the thought of death. St. Jane made this statement: "I am so violently attacked that I do not know what to do to defend my soul. At times it seems that I can bear no more and that I am just about ready to give up everything. The temptations are so cruel and unending that I would welcome death at any hour of the day. Sometimes I can neither eat nor sleep."

God's assistance, however, never really failed her; but to her it seemed that God had abandoned her, for she no longer found the least satisfaction, but rather tediousness and anguish, in prayer, in the reading of spiritual books, in receiving Communion and in all other devout practices. The only thing she could do in her desolation was to look at her God and let Him do with her what He pleased.

This is the way in which God makes saints.

All sanctity consists in loving God, and all love of God consists in doing His will.

So — love God and do what you please; for if you sincerely love God, the only thing that will please you is doing God's will.

PRAYER

Jesus, You are the only hope and love of my soul. I do not deserve Your consolations and tenderness. I neither deserve them nor ask for them. But I do ask this favor: make me love You; make me do Your holy will as long as I live, and then do with me what You please.

I love You, Jesus, with all my heart. I love You more than myself. I desire nothing in this life but to love You. I understand well that even my good desire to love You is a gift of Your grace. My Lord, perfect the work; help me always until my death. Do not leave me to myself. Give me grace to overcome all temptations and to conquer myself. To gain this grace help me to pray always and to recommend myself to You.

I desire to be all Yours. I give You my body, my soul, my will, my freedom. I wish no longer to live for myself, but only for You, my God and my all. I want to become holy as You want me to be. I hope for Your help.

O Mary, hope of sinners, you are so powerful with God. I have great confidence in your intercession. I beg you, by the love you bear to Jesus, help me! Help me always to love God and to keep on loving Him forever.

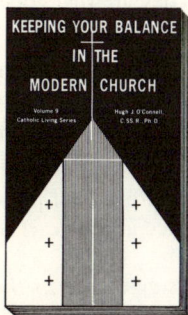